AF506849

Teaching What Every Employer Wants

Employability Skills in Every CTE Classroom

Dr. Ben Clinton

Teaching What Every Employer Wants

Employability Skills in Every CTE Classroom

Copyright © 2026 Benjamin Clinton

All rights reserved.

No part of this book may be reproduced, distributed, or transmitted in any form or by any means, electronic or mechanical, including photocopying, recording, or by any information storage and retrieval system, without the prior written permission of the publisher, except in the case of brief quotations embodied in critical reviews and certain other noncommercial uses permitted by copyright law.

Published by Beacon Education Press

An imprint of Beacon Administrative Consulting

Printed in the United States of America

First edition

ISBN 979-8-9945410-0-5 (paperback)

ISBN 979-8-9945410-0-2 (e-book)

The views and opinions expressed in this book are those of the author and do not necessarily reflect the official policies or positions of any school district, institution, organization, or employer referenced. Examples and case studies are presented for educational purposes only.

All trademarks referenced in this book are the property of their respective owners. Their use does not imply endorsement.

For the teachers who stayed, and the students who were capable long before they knew it.

Foreword

by Julian Alvarez III, Former Commissioner Representing Labor, Texas Workforce Commission (2016–2022)

For six years, I had the honor of serving as the Commissioner Representing Labor at the Texas Workforce Commission, advocating for more than 14 million workers across our state. In that role, and in the years before and after it, I met employers, educators, and community leaders from every corner of Texas. No matter the industry or the region, one truth surfaced again and again:

Employers consistently tell us that technical skills matter, but they aren't enough on their own. What's proving hardest to find are individuals who can communicate, collaborate, show up ready to work, solve problems, and keep growing.

Those aren't "extra" skills. They are the foundation of a strong workforce and, frankly, the foundation of a strong economy.

That's why this book matters.

In *Teaching What Every Employer Wants*, Dr. Ben Clinton captures something I saw repeatedly during my time at TWC: Texas students are talented and capable, but they need intentional support to develop the employability skills that carry them from the classroom to a successful career.

What stands out in this book is that it isn't theoretical. Dr. Clinton brings together voices from teachers, workforce leaders, industry professionals, and real employers, from construction to healthcare to tech. He includes insights from innovative programs like UTRGV's Career Bridge, which is redefining how students gain real-world skills before they ever enter the workforce.

He approaches employability skills the same way employers do: as essential, teachable, and measurable behaviors that determine professional success.

This book gives educators a practical roadmap they can apply in *any* CTE pathway, because the same core skills are demanded everywhere. Whether a student becomes a welder, a nurse, a programmer, or a manager, the expectations remain the same: communicate well, act professionally, take initiative, manage your time, solve problems, and work well with others.

During my years at TWC, we pushed hard to expand apprenticeships, strengthen work-based learning, and connect classrooms with industry. We knew that Texas' economic future depended on students who were not only technically prepared, but work-ready. Dr. Clinton is carrying that mission forward.

He has taken a message employers have been saying for decades and translated it into a guide educators can use every single day to shape the next generation of Texas workers.

If you are a teacher, a CTE leader, or anyone responsible for preparing young people for their futures, this book will give you tools, perspective, and a renewed sense of purpose.

Texas needs a skilled workforce.

But more than that, it needs a prepared workforce.

Students who can lead, contribute, and adapt in every environment they enter.

This book helps make that possible.

Julian Alvarez III

Former Commissioner Representing Labor

Texas Workforce Commission (2016–2022)

Acknowledgements

This book reflects the work and wisdom of many people, even though the responsibility for its words is mine alone.

First, to the CTE teachers I have worked with over the years. You opened your classrooms, shared your frustrations, tested ideas, and kept showing up for students even when the work was heavy and the recognition was light. Much of what appears in these pages comes directly from watching you coach, redirect, encourage, and refuse to lower the bar. This book exists because of your professionalism.

To the employers and industry partners who spoke honestly about what they see and what they need. Thank you for your candor and your patience with education. Your willingness to name the gap, without dismissing the people trying to close it, made this work possible.

To Eloy Garza and the UTRGV students participating in the RGV LEAD Innovation Hub, thank you for trusting me with your story. The Student-Led Agency model you built, supported by Career Bridge, demonstrates how real responsibility reshapes how students see themselves and their work. The students' reflections, especially those shared with honesty and clarity, anchor this book in lived experience rather than theory.

To Patrick Anthony and the leaders across construction, healthcare, information technology, and hospitality who shared their experiences, thank you for grounding this work in reality. Your stories confirmed what educators often sense but do not always hear validated.

To Julian Alvarez, former Workforce Commissioner, thank you for your leadership and for contributing the foreword to this book. Your perspective bridges education and workforce in a way few voices can, and your support reinforces why this conversation matters beyond any single classroom or program.

To the campus and district leaders I have learned from, including those who challenged my thinking when it needed it, thank you for reminding me that culture is built through habits, not slogans.

Finally, to my family. Thank you for your patience during early mornings, late nights, and long conversations that spilled beyond work hours. Your support made the space for this book to be written.

This book is ultimately about helping students succeed in the real world. It is also about honoring the educators and leaders who keep believing that how we teach matters just as much as what we teach.

Table of Contents

Introduction: *Why Technical Skill Is Not Enough*

Every year, students leave CTE classrooms with certifications, credentials, and technical skills that look strong on paper. And every year, too many of those same students struggle to keep jobs, grow in roles, or earn the trust of the people around them.

The issue is rarely whether students can do the work. It is whether they know how to work.

They struggle with communication. They avoid feedback. They miss deadlines. They shut down when things get difficult. They wait to be told instead of stepping forward. These are not technical failures. They are employability failures.

Most educators already recognize this. Teachers coach students through group conflict, remind them to show up prepared, and model professionalism in moments that never appear on a lesson plan. Much of the most important work happening in schools is behavioral, relational, and rarely named.

This book exists to name it.

It is not a critique of schools, teachers, or students. It is an acknowledgment of reality. Technical skills open doors. Employability skills determine what happens once students walk through them.

Over more than two decades in education, including more than fifteen years overseeing CTE programs, I have watched students succeed and stall for reasons that had nothing to do with ability. I have seen new teachers with deep technical expertise struggle until they developed communication and leadership skills. I have watched campuses improve when leaders focused less on programs and more on habits.

I have also spent years listening to employers across industries. Construction. Healthcare. Technology. Hospitality. Small businesses. Global firms. Different settings. The same message.

We can teach the technical work.

We struggle to teach how to show up.

CTE classrooms are uniquely positioned to close that gap. They already resemble the workplace. They already operate around projects, deadlines, teamwork, and accountability. The challenge is not adding something new. It is teaching what is already there with intention.

I realized how far this idea could reach during a conversation with a high school principal I worked closely with, Mr. Amaya. I shared an early version of this framework with him, framed entirely around CTE. He listened carefully, nodded, and then paused.

"Why are we only doing this with CTE teachers?" he asked.

"These are the skills every teacher is trying to build."

He was right.

Employability skills do not belong to one pathway. They show up anywhere students are asked to work with others, manage themselves, communicate clearly, and follow through. The difference in CTE is not relevance, but visibility. These habits are easier to see, easier to name, and easier to practice in classrooms built around real work.

This book is written for CTE teachers because they are already doing much of this work, often without shared language or tools. It is also written with campus and district leaders in mind, and for any educator who recognizes that preparation for life after school is as much about behavior as it is about content.

You will not find slogans here. You will not find a program to adopt. You will find a clear framework, real examples, and practical tools that help students build habits they will carry long after they forget specific lessons.

This is a book about employability, not as an add-on, but as the foundation that makes everything else matter.

How to Use This Book

This book is not meant to be read like a manual, and it is not meant to be implemented all at once.

Some readers will start at the beginning and read straight through. Others will jump to the sections that feel most urgent. Both approaches are valid.

If you are new to employability skills work, start with Part I. It provides language and context that will make the rest of the book easier to use.

If you want to hear directly from employers and industry leaders, Part II grounds the conversation in real expectations and real consequences.

If you are looking for classroom strategies you can use immediately, Part III is designed for you. These chapters focus on routines, lesson integration, assessment, and student support without adding unnecessary complexity.

Part IV is a toolkit. Use it selectively. Adapt what fits. Ignore what does not. These tools are meant to support your judgment, not replace it.

Part V brings the work together. It speaks directly to teachers, leaders, and students, and offers a clear path forward without asking you to do everything at once.

You do not need to agree with every example or use every tool for this book to be useful. The goal is not fidelity. The goal is clarity.

If this book helps you name what you are already doing, adjust one routine, or coach one student more intentionally, it has done its job.

Part I

The Foundation

Before we talk about strategies, tools, or classroom routines, we need a shared understanding of what we mean by employability skills and how they function in real workplaces.

Employability skills are often treated as supplemental. Important, but secondary. Something addressed after content is covered and certifications are earned. In practice, they operate differently. Employability skills are the conditions under which technical skills matter. They shape how students apply what they know, communicate what they understand, and respond when expectations shift.

These skills influence how students are perceived, trusted, and developed once they enter the workforce. They determine whether technical ability translates into reliability, growth, and long-term opportunity.

This section defines employability skills clearly and places them in a real-world context. It examines the gap between how readiness is often measured in schools and how it is experienced by employers. It introduces the core skills this book focuses on and explains why they appear consistently across industries, roles, and levels of responsibility.

This section also frames why career and technical education is uniquely positioned to lead this work. CTE classrooms already reflect the rhythms of the workplace. They rely on projects, deadlines, collaboration, and accountability. The opportunity is not relevance, but intention. Making these expectations explicit, teachable, and repeatable.

Finally, this section explains why this book exists and how it is organized. The chapters that follow move from definition to evidence, from culture to practice, and from tools to application.

Part I establishes the foundation. Everything that follows is built on it.

Chapter 1

What Every Employer Wants

Let's start with the obvious. Employers want people who can do the job. They want mechanics who can diagnose a problem and fix the vehicle. Welders who can lay a clean bead. Dental assistants who know how to prep a tray, manage the room, and put a nervous patient at ease. Technical skill matters. Certifications matter. Nobody is arguing otherwise.

But spend enough time talking to employers and another frustration surfaces quickly. They are not just struggling to find skilled workers. They are struggling to keep them. And that problem has very little to do with tools, textbooks, or training manuals.

"We can teach someone how to weld," one supervisor told me. "But can we teach them to show up on time, take feedback, and keep their phone in their pocket?"

I have heard that sentence, or some version of it, for more than a decade. Manufacturing, healthcare, construction, IT, hospitality, education. The industry changes, but the concern does not. And if you have worked with students for more than a few minutes, you have probably had the same thought yourself.

For a long time, we defined career readiness in simple terms. Earn a certification. Build a resume. Practice interview questions. Send students on their way. Those things still matter. They always will. But today's workforce expects more, and not more content. More maturity.

Employers are looking for people who can communicate without shutting down or lashing out. People who can work with others even when it is uncomfortable. People who notice problems and act instead of waiting. People who manage their time, their emotions, and their attention. In short, they want the full package. Someone who can do the job and function as part of a team.

This is where many young people struggle.

A recent Newsweek article reported that six out of ten employers had let go of a Gen Z hire due to performance issues. Not because those employees could not learn the work, but because they struggled with behaviors tied to work itself. Showing up consistently. Taking direction. Staying engaged through stress, boredom, or criticism.

The National Association of Colleges and Employers surveys hiring managers every year, and their priorities rarely change. Problem solving. Teamwork. Communication. Work ethic. Initiative and flexibility. None of these are technical skills, and none of them are optional.

Listen closely to how employers talk when they stop being polite. They are not asking for perfection. They are asking for reliability. Someone who shows up early and ready to work. Someone who does not fall apart when things go wrong. Someone who can take feedback without getting defensive. Someone who stays off their phone and figures things out instead of waiting to be told.

These are not bonus traits. They are deal breakers.

I once visited a manufacturing plant that hosted summer interns from a local high school. The plant manager, Mr. Davis, was a former Marine. Direct, observant, and clear about expectations. He told me about one student who looked perfect on paper. Strong grades. Solid technical knowledge. Comfortable with CAD software. Confident in interviews.

"He nailed the technical part," Davis said. "But by week two, we had problems."

The student showed up late, missed instructions, and did not ask for help when he got stuck. When corrected, he brushed it off. Eventually, they had to let him go. "He knew the tools," Davis explained, "but he did not know how to be part of a team. If someone ignores safety or misses deadlines, it affects everyone."

Then Davis told me about another intern. A young woman who struggled more with the machinery at first but showed up early, took notes, asked questions, and cleaned up her area without being asked. She stayed late when needed. She was offered a part time job before the internship ended.

"We can teach the rest," Davis said. "We just need the attitude."

A CTE teacher once shared a similar story with me about a senior in her welding program. The student was technically strong and passed every certification exam. He was also argumentative, dismissive of peers, and careless about cleaning his workspace. His confidence in his skill had blinded him to the impact of his behavior.

She finally sat him down and said what most people avoid. "If I were your boss, I would fire you. Your welding isn't the problem. Your attitude is."

It was not comfortable, but it was honest. Two years later, that student messaged her from his first jobsite. "Thank you," he wrote. "I finally get it."

That moment is why this work matters.

Teaching employability skills is not just CTE's responsibility. Families, schools, communities, and employers all play a role. But CTE classrooms are uniquely positioned to lead this work. Your students are already managing projects, sharing equipment, meeting deadlines, and solving problems under pressure. What happens in your lab already looks and feels like the workplace.

That makes behaviors visible, and therefore teachable.

The mistake is assuming students will pick these skills up automatically. Some will. Many will not. Just like technical skills, employability skills require instruction, feedback, practice, and repetition. Hope is not a strategy.

Take a moment for an honest self-check. Are expectations around time, teamwork, and communication explicitly taught, or only enforced after something goes wrong? Do students reflect on how they work, or only on the grade they earn? Are accountability and professionalism modeled daily, or only discussed when there is a problem?

This book is not about adding another program, unit, or initiative. It is about helping you teach what employers already expect, using what you already do. You will learn how to embed employability skills into daily routines, assess behavior without becoming the behavior police, support students who struggle with motivation or maturity, and partner with employers in ways that actually help students grow.

You do not need to be a motivational speaker. You do not need a separate soft skills class. You do not need more hours in the day. You need simple, repeatable strategies that fit your classroom, your shop, and your reality.

If you have ever had a student who was almost ready, this book is for you. The next step is getting clear about what these skills really are and how to teach them on purpose.

Chapter 2

What We Mean When We Say "Employability Skills"

Let's get specific.

If you've heard the phrase *soft skills* more times than you can count, you've probably asked yourself a reasonable question: what does that actually look like in my classroom? Not in theory. Not on a poster. On a Tuesday afternoon when half your class is tired and the other half wants to be anywhere else.

You're not alone in asking that.

I once led a training where a welding instructor raised his hand and said, "I get that these skills matter, but how do I teach a kid not to be lazy?"

The room laughed, because the question was blunt. But it was also honest. He wasn't asking for new terminology or another framework. He was asking for something practical. Something he could use the next day in his shop, with the students standing in front of him. He was naming a frustration most teachers feel but rarely say out loud.

That question captures the real tension around employability skills. Educators are not confused about whether these behaviors matter. They see the impact every day. What they struggle with is how to address them in a way that feels fair, teachable, and connected to learning, rather than reactive or disciplinary.

No teacher wants to spend their day lecturing students about attitude. No one wants to turn every correction into a character judgment. And no one believes that effort, responsibility, or professionalism can simply be demanded into existence.

What teachers are really asking is this: how do I help students develop habits that matter at work without losing the integrity of my instruction or the relationships in my classroom?

That is the gap this chapter is meant to address.

When the Language Gets in the Way

Part of the confusion comes from the language itself.

We hear *soft skills, employability skills, professional skills, workplace readiness, 21st century skills*. Different labels, same general idea. These terms are meant to capture the habits and behaviors that allow people to function, contribute, and grow in a workplace.

But the language often works against the work.

Calling these skills "soft" makes them sound optional or secondary, as if they matter less than technical knowledge. Framing them as "professionalism" can feel vague or moralizing. Talking about "workplace readiness" can make them sound like something that happens later, somewhere else, after the real teaching is done.

None of that matches what teachers actually see.

In CTE classrooms especially, these behaviors are not abstract. They are visible and constant. They show up in how students talk to one another, how they handle frustration, how they manage time, and how they respond when something goes wrong. They surface in group work, in cleanup routines, in safety conversations, and in moments when a student has to decide whether to step up or check out.

And because these behaviors are always present, teachers are already responding to them. They redirect tone. They address missed deadlines. They step into group conflict. They coach students through moments that never appear on a lesson plan. Much of this work happens quietly, instinctively, and without a shared language to support it.

The challenge is not awareness. The challenge is coherence.

When behaviors are corrected but not named, students experience them as personal. When expectations are enforced inconsistently, students see them as arbitrary. When employability skills are discussed only after something goes wrong, they feel like punishment instead of preparation.

This is where language matters. Not as jargon, but as clarity.

Before we define employability skills, before we assess them, and before we build systems around them, we need a shared understanding of what we are actually talking about. Not as a checklist or a list of traits, but as patterns of behavior that already shape outcomes in every classroom.

That framing sets the stage for what comes next.

You've Seen This Person Before

Let me put this in more familiar terms.

Think about someone you've worked with who was technically strong. They knew the material. They could pass the certification exam. On paper, they checked every box. And yet, working with them was exhausting.

Maybe they missed deadlines and always had a reason. Maybe they bristled at feedback or shut down when things didn't go their way. Maybe they did exactly what was asked and nothing more, even when the situation clearly called for judgment or initiative. Over time, you stopped relying on them. The skills were there. Trust wasn't.

Now think about the opposite.

Someone who may not have been the most technically polished at first, but who listened carefully, asked questions, followed through, and adjusted when things went wrong. Someone you trusted with responsibility because they took ownership of their work and their impact on others.

Most employers will tell you the same thing: they can train technical gaps faster than they can change habits.

This is the heart of what we mean by employability skills. They are not personality traits. They are not about likability or compliance. They are the behaviors that make skill usable in real environments where people depend on one another.

In classrooms, we often separate learning from behavior. Content lives in one lane. Conduct lives in another. But workplaces don't make that distinction. The way someone communicates, manages time, responds to feedback, and works with others directly affects outcomes. Those behaviors are part of the work, not distractions from it.

When students struggle in jobs, internships, or apprenticeships, it's rarely because they forgot the technical steps. It's because something else got in the way. Miscommunication. Missed expectations. Poor follow through. Difficulty navigating conflict or ambiguity. Students don't always see that connection on their own. That's not a flaw. It's a developmental gap. And it's one schools are uniquely positioned to address, if we are willing to name it clearly and teach it intentionally.

What Employability Skills Actually Are

Employability skills are best understood as observable behaviors, not abstract qualities.

They are what students do when the instructions are unclear. How they respond when feedback is uncomfortable. Whether they follow through when no one is checking closely. Whether they adjust when the plan changes or the group dynamic shifts.

These skills are not separate from technical learning. They operate alongside it, shaping how effectively knowledge is applied. A student may know the correct procedure, but if they cannot communicate a problem, collaborate with a team, or manage their time under pressure, that knowledge stays locked in place.

This is why employability skills are already being practiced every day, whether we call them that or not.

When a student explains a lab process to a partner, they are practicing communication. When a group negotiates roles and responsibilities, they are practicing collaboration. When a student realizes they are behind and has to decide whether to ask for help or cut corners, they are practicing professional judgment.

The difference is whether those moments are made visible.

When employability skills remain unnamed, students experience them as isolated corrections. When they are named and reinforced, students begin to see patterns. They start to understand that how they work matters just as much as what they produce.

This shift is subtle, but powerful. It moves conversations away from character judgments and toward professional expectations. Instead of "you're being lazy," the conversation becomes "this task required follow through, and the follow through didn't happen." Instead of "you have a bad attitude," it becomes "the way you responded made collaboration harder."

That language matters. It gives students something concrete to improve, rather than something personal to defend.

Most importantly, it aligns classroom expectations with workplace reality. Employers don't evaluate effort based on intention. They evaluate it based on impact. Teaching students to recognize that distinction early prepares them for environments where accountability is real and feedback is continuous.

This is not about adding more to your plate. It's about sharpening what you already do.

Next, we'll look at how these behaviors show up naturally in CTE environments and why those settings are uniquely suited to teach employability skills without turning them into a separate program or curriculum.

Why CTE Classrooms Are the Advantage

Career and Technical Education classrooms already contain the conditions most schools struggle to manufacture.

Work is visible. Time matters. Mistakes have consequences. Equipment is shared. Processes depend on sequence and coordination. Outcomes are tangible. These environments naturally expose the behaviors that determine whether someone can function in a real workplace.

In a traditional academic setting, it's often possible for students to succeed quietly and independently. In a CTE setting, learning happens out loud. How a student shows up affects everyone else in the room. A missed step can delay a project. Poor communication can create safety risks. Lack of follow through doesn't just lower a grade; it disrupts the workflow.

That's not a weakness. It's the opportunity.

When students work in shops, labs, kitchens, studios, and simulated workplaces, employability skills surface whether we intend them to or not. The question is whether those moments are treated as interruptions or as instruction.

Too often, behavior issues are handled quickly so the class can "get back to content." A late arrival is corrected and forgotten. A missed deadline is penalized and moved past. A group conflict is resolved just enough to keep things moving.

But those are the moments when employability skills are actually being taught.

CTE teachers already manage professional environments. They enforce safety standards. They set production expectations. They coach students through mistakes. With a slight shift in framing, those same actions become explicit lessons in professionalism, accountability, communication, and judgment.

This is why employability skills don't need a separate unit or poster campaign. They need recognition.

When students understand that these behaviors are part of the work, not distractions from it, they begin to take them seriously. They stop seeing corrections as personal and start seeing them as professional. That shift alone changes how feedback is received and applied.

CTE classrooms don't need to become something else to teach employability skills. They need to lean more fully into what they already are.

Making the Implicit Explicit

The difference between teaching employability skills accidentally and teaching them intentionally comes down to language and consistency.

When expectations are assumed, students guess. When expectations are named, students learn.

Consider how often students hear vague feedback. "Be more responsible." "Act more professional." "Take this seriously." Those statements may be accurate, but they aren't instructional. They don't tell students what to do differently next time.

Now contrast that with feedback tied to observable behavior. "You missed two check-ins and didn't communicate why." "The way you spoke to your teammate shut down the conversation." "This task required follow through after the initial work was done, and that didn't happen."

Those statements point to specific actions. They give students something to practice.

This approach does not lower expectations. It clarifies them.

Students don't always know what professionalism looks like in context. Many have never been in environments where expectations were explicit, consistent, and connected to real outcomes. When we assume they should already know, we miss the chance to teach.

Intentional employability instruction lives in the margins of daily work. It shows up in how routines are framed, how feedback is delivered, and how reflection is guided.

A missed deadline becomes a conversation about planning and communication, not just points lost. A group conflict becomes a discussion about collaboration and accountability, not just behavior management. A strong performance becomes an opportunity to name what worked and why it mattered.

Over time, patterns emerge. Students begin to anticipate expectations instead of reacting to them. They adjust their behavior before being corrected. They take ownership not because they are told to, but because they understand the consequences of not doing so.

That is when employability skills stop feeling like an add-on.

They become part of the job.

In the next chapter, we'll look at the specific employability skills employers consistently name, and what those expectations actually sound like when they are applied to real work.

Chapter 3

The Ten Employability Skills Employers Expect

When employers talk about "soft skills," they are rarely speaking in abstract terms. They're describing behaviors they see, or don't see, every day. The way a new hire responds to feedback. How they manage time when things get busy. Whether they notice a problem and act, or wait to be told.

This chapter breaks down ten employability skills employers consistently identify as essential. Not as buzzwords, but as habits you can recognize, teach, and reinforce in real settings. These skills show up differently across industries, but the core behaviors remain the same.

Each section that follows names the behavior, shows how it appears in classrooms, and explains why employers notice it so quickly.

1. Communication

Communication is the ability to give and receive information clearly, completely, and respectfully. It includes speaking, listening, writing, and nonverbal cues, but at its core, communication is about alignment. Do people understand what is expected, what happened, and what needs to happen next? When communication breaks down, everything else follows.

In the workplace, poor communication costs time, money, and trust. Instructions get missed. Safety steps get skipped. Problems compound because no one asked a clarifying question early enough. Employers do not expect polished speakers or perfect grammar. They expect clarity, honesty, and the ability to listen without defensiveness.

In classrooms, communication shows up constantly, whether we name it or not. Students practice it when they explain a process to a partner, clarify a safety step before starting a task, or give peer feedback without sarcasm or dismissal. They practice it when they listen closely the first time instead of asking for directions to be repeated, and when they speak up early rather than waiting until a mistake has already been made.

You also see communication breakdown in familiar ways. A student nods along without really understanding. Another reacts emotionally to feedback instead of asking questions. A group struggles when expectations were never stated clearly. These moments are not interruptions to learning. They are the learning.

In the workplace, communication looks like a technician explaining an issue to a customer without blaming the equipment, a dental assistant accurately relaying patient concerns to a provider, or a welder speaking up about a safety risk before it becomes an accident. Employers notice quickly who communicates to avoid responsibility and who communicates to solve problems.

What makes communication an employability skill is not the act of talking. It is the habit of checking for understanding, adjusting tone, and choosing clarity over convenience. When students learn that how they communicate affects safety, efficiency, and trust, the skill stops being abstract. It becomes necessary.

2. Collaboration and Teamwork

Collaboration is the ability to work effectively with others toward a shared goal. It requires shared responsibility, flexibility, and the willingness to contribute even when the work is uncomfortable or inconvenient. Teamwork is not about liking the people you work with. It is about functioning well with them.

In the workplace, very little work happens in isolation. Jobs that appear independent from the outside still rely on coordination, timing, and trust. When teamwork breaks down, the cost is immediate. Work slows. Mistakes multiply. Frustration rises. Employers notice quickly when someone cannot function as part of a team, even if that person is technically strong.

CTE classrooms mirror this reality more closely than most academic settings. Students share tools, space, time, and outcomes. They depend on each other to complete builds, rotate stations, and meet deadlines. Collaboration becomes visible when roles are clear and accountability is shared. It breaks down when one student carries the load, others disengage, or conflict is avoided instead of addressed.

Many students struggle with teamwork because they have never been taught how to work through it. They do not know how to clarify roles, address tension, or give feedback without escalating conflict. Left unaddressed, these moments become behavioral issues. Addressed intentionally, they become employability lessons.

In the workplace, collaboration looks like coordinated handoffs, shared responsibility, and professional disagreement handled without drama. Auto service teams rely on timing and trust. Healthcare staff coordinate patient care across shifts. Construction crews depend on each other's precision and follow through. Employers value workers who communicate openly, contribute consistently, and resolve problems without making them personal.

The teaching opportunity lies in naming what is already happening. When students reflect on how their actions affected the group, teamwork stops being a vague expectation and becomes a measurable behavior. They begin to see that collaboration is not about fairness in effort, but about reliability in contribution.

Strong teamwork is built when students understand that their work affects more than their grade. It affects the group's progress, the quality of the outcome, and the trust others place in them. When that connection is made, collaboration becomes real, not because it is enforced, but because it matters.

3. Time Management

Time management is the ability to plan, prioritize, and complete work within real constraints. It is not about working faster. It is about working intentionally. Knowing how long something takes, sequencing tasks appropriately, and staying focused long enough to finish without cutting corners.

In the workplace, poor time management rarely announces itself as a character flaw. It shows up as missed deadlines, rushed work, unfinished tasks, and preventable stress. Employers do not expect employees to work nonstop. They expect them to manage time well enough that the work gets done safely, accurately, and on schedule.

In classrooms, time management often hides behind other issues. A student who rushes at the end of class. One who leaves cleanup unfinished. A group that runs out of time not because the task was too hard, but because they misjudged how long it would take. These are not motivation problems. They are planning problems.

CTE classrooms already provide natural opportunities to teach this skill. Students rotate through stations, manage shared equipment, work within class periods, and balance production with cleanup. When those routines are treated as instructional moments instead of enforcement moments, students begin to understand time as a resource, not a threat.

In the workplace, time management determines productivity, safety, and customer trust. A technician must meet flat rate expectations without skipping steps. A cosmetology student must manage multiple clients without falling behind. A welder must balance quality with deadlines. In professional settings, the impact is immediate.

What makes time management an employability skill is not speed. It is judgment. The ability to slow down when precision matters and move efficiently when it doesn't. When students learn to estimate, adjust, and follow through, time stops being something that happens to them. It becomes something they can manage.

4. Critical Thinking

Critical thinking is the ability to slow down, assess what is happening, and make sound judgments before acting. It is not about having the right answer immediately. It is about asking the right questions first.

In classrooms, critical thinking shows up when students pause to understand why something isn't working instead of rushing to fix it. It appears when they examine instructions carefully, notice patterns, question assumptions, and consider multiple options before choosing a path forward. These habits often develop quietly, but they are foundational.

CTE environments naturally demand critical thinking because conditions are rarely perfect. Measurements vary. Materials behave differently than expected. Instructions leave room for interpretation.

Students must decide what information matters, what can be ignored, and what requires further clarification. When teachers name these moments as thinking work, students begin to recognize that judgment is part of the task, not separate from it.

In the workplace, critical thinking allows employees to avoid costly mistakes. Employers rely on workers who can evaluate situations, anticipate consequences, and make informed decisions without constant supervision. This is especially important in environments where safety, quality, and efficiency depend on sound judgment.

Critical thinking also requires humility. Strong thinkers recognize when they need more information. They ask questions before acting. They seek feedback when uncertainty remains. This willingness to think carefully instead of reacting impulsively builds credibility over time.

When students develop critical thinking skills, they become less dependent on step-by-step instructions and more capable of navigating complexity. Employers notice employees who can interpret situations, weigh options, and make decisions that hold up under pressure. That capability signals readiness long before technical mastery does.

5. Initiative

Initiative is the difference between waiting and acting. It is the habit that signals ownership before anyone asks for it. Employers notice initiative quickly, because it reduces friction everywhere it shows up.

When employers talk about initiative, they are not asking for people who overstep boundaries or constantly try to impress. They are looking for workers who notice what needs to be done and take responsibility for it. Someone who asks a clarifying question instead of guessing. Someone who restocks supplies without being reminded. Someone who steps in to help a teammate who is falling behind because the work matters, not because they are chasing recognition.

In classrooms, initiative often gets misunderstood. Students who act independently are sometimes labeled as bossy or impatient. Others are hesitant to act at all because they have learned that school rewards compliance more than ownership. Over time, many students become very good at waiting. Waiting for instructions. Waiting for reminders. Waiting for permission.

That habit is costly once expectations shift.

Employers consistently describe frustration with new hires who technically know what to do but require constant prompting to do it. They see potential, but they also see passivity. Initiative signals something deeper than motivation. It signals engagement. It tells an employer that someone is paying attention to the work, the environment, and the people around them.

CTE classrooms already create natural opportunities for initiative to surface. Shared equipment needs to be cleaned. Materials need to be prepped. Timelines need to be managed. Teammates need support. The difference is whether those moments are framed intentionally. When students understand that noticing and acting are part of the job, initiative stops feeling optional.

Initiative also grows when students are allowed to make decisions and experience the results. If every step is prescribed, there is no reason to step forward. When students are trusted with responsibility, even in small ways, they begin to see themselves as contributors rather than participants.

Over time, initiative becomes a habit. Students stop asking what they are supposed to do next and start asking what would help the work move forward. That shift changes how they are perceived, not just in class, but everywhere responsibility exists.

Initiative is not about doing more work. It is about taking ownership of the work that already exists.

6. Professionalism

Professionalism is often treated as a vague expectation, something students are supposed to "just know" once they leave school. In reality, it is one of the most concrete and observable employability skills employers evaluate, and one of the fastest ways new hires either earn trust or lose it.

Employers rarely define professionalism in abstract terms. They describe it through behaviors. Does this person show up when they say they will? Do they take responsibility when something goes wrong? Do they accept feedback without becoming defensive, sarcastic, or disengaged? Do they respect the people, tools, and environment around them? These are not personality traits. They are patterns of behavior that signal whether someone is ready to function in a professional setting.

In CTE classrooms, professionalism shows up long before students ever step into a job. It appears in how they arrive to class, how they handle equipment, how they speak to peers, and how they respond when corrected. It is visible in whether safety protocols are followed consistently or only when an instructor is watching. It shows up in tone, body language, and attention, especially when tasks feel routine or uninteresting.

The challenge is that professionalism is often enforced only after it breaks down. A student is late repeatedly, and a consequence follows. A student talks back, and the conversation turns disciplinary. Phones appear, and rules are restated. When professionalism is framed primarily through correction, students learn how to avoid getting in trouble rather than how to build habits that carry into the workplace.

Employers experience professionalism differently. There is rarely a warning phase. Expectations are assumed, not negotiated. A missed deadline affects a customer. A careless comment damages trust. A defensive response to feedback signals risk. New hires are not judged on isolated moments, but on patterns. Consistency matters more than intent.

This is where classrooms can do more than prepare students academically. They can make professionalism visible, teachable, and routine. When expectations are named clearly and reinforced consistently, students begin to understand that professionalism is not about compliance or personality. It is about reliability.

That reliability grows when students are expected to take responsibility for how their behavior affects others. Wearing the right gear is no longer just about following a rule; it's about protecting a team. Communicating clearly is not about sounding polite; it's about preventing mistakes. Accepting feedback without deflection is not about submission; it's about improving performance.

Professionalism also develops when students are allowed to recover. In real workplaces, people make mistakes. What matters is how they respond. Classrooms that coach students through missteps, rather than simply penalizing them, teach a more accurate lesson about professional growth. Accountability paired with guidance builds maturity. Punishment alone builds avoidance.

Over time, students begin to internalize these expectations. They stop asking what the minimum is and start considering how their actions reflect on their work, their team, and themselves. That shift changes how they show up, not just in class, but everywhere responsibility is expected.

Professionalism is not about turning classrooms into offices or stripping learning of humanity. It is about helping students practice the behaviors that allow skills to matter. When professionalism becomes part of the daily work, students leave with more than technical competence. They leave with credibility.

And credibility is what opens doors long after the interview ends.

7. Adaptability

Adaptability is the ability to adjust without losing effectiveness. It is not about liking change. It is about responding to it with control, flexibility, and forward motion.

In the workplace, change is constant. Schedules shift. Technology updates. Materials arrive late. Customers change their minds. Employers do not expect workers to enjoy these disruptions, but they do expect them to respond without shutting down, lashing out, or giving up.

Adaptability shows up in how someone handles the moment after a plan stops working.

In classrooms, adaptability is often tested quietly. A group member is absent. Equipment is unavailable. Instructions change mid-task. These moments reveal whether students can regroup or whether they become stuck, frustrated, or disengaged. The difference is rarely intelligence. It is emotional regulation and flexibility.

CTE environments provide natural pressure points for adaptability because the work is physical, time-bound, and often unpredictable. When students are coached to pause, reassess, and adjust rather than react, they begin to develop habits that transfer directly to the workplace.

Adaptability does not replace planning or problem solving. It supports them. Planning assumes things will go as expected. Adaptability prepares students for when they do not. Employers value workers who can recover quickly, stay professional under pressure, and continue moving forward even when conditions are less than ideal.

Adaptability also grows through reflection. When students are asked what changed, how they responded, and what they would do differently next time, they begin to see adjustment as a skill rather than a failure.

Over time, adaptable students stop being derailed by disruption. They learn to respond with calm, flexibility, and purpose. That steadiness is one of the clearest signals of readiness employers look for, especially in fast moving environments.

8. Problem Solving

Problem solving is the ability to move from recognizing an issue to taking effective action. It turns awareness into response.

Where critical thinking focuses on analysis and judgment, problem solving shows up in what someone does next. It is the habit of attempting solutions instead of freezing, guessing, or immediately handing the issue to someone else.

In classrooms, problem solving appears when equipment malfunctions, measurements are off, materials run out, or results do not match expectations. These moments are where learning becomes unavoidable. Students are forced to diagnose what went wrong, decide what to try, and adjust based on results.

CTE settings make this visible because problems have consequences. A bad cut wastes material. A missed step affects safety. A delayed decision slows the whole team. When students are coached to work through problems rather than around them, they begin to build confidence in their ability to recover.

In the workplace, employers value problem solvers because they reduce downtime and prevent small issues from becoming larger ones. Effective problem solvers do not panic or deflect responsibility. They assess the situation, attempt a reasonable solution, communicate clearly, and escalate only when needed.

Problem solving also requires follow through. Fixing the immediate issue is not enough. Strong problem solvers reflect on what caused the problem and adjust their approach to prevent it from happening again.

When students develop this habit, they stop waiting for rescue. They learn that struggle is part of work and that their response matters more than the mistake itself. That shift builds reliability, confidence, and trust.

Over time, problem solving becomes less about fixing things and more about how students approach uncertainty. Employers notice those who engage problems directly, think through options, and act with intention. That behavior signals readiness far more clearly than technical accuracy alone.

9. Work Ethic

Work ethic is often described as effort, but effort alone is not what employers are looking for. Work ethic is reliability over time. It is the pattern of showing up, following through, and caring about the quality of work even when conditions are not ideal.

In classrooms, work ethic shows up in persistence. Students with strong work ethic finish what they start. They revise when needed. They stay engaged when tasks become repetitive or challenging. They do not disappear when things get difficult.

What makes work ethic hard to teach is that it cannot be reduced to enthusiasm or personality. A quiet student can have strong work ethic. A confident student can lack it. Employers are not measuring energy. They are measuring consistency.

CTE environments make work ethic visible because the work itself has consequences. A rushed weld fails inspection. A missed step creates a safety risk. An incomplete project affects the entire team.

When expectations are clear, students begin to see that effort is not just about trying hard. It is about meeting standards consistently.

In the workplace, work ethic builds trust. Employers invest time and training in people who demonstrate reliability. They hesitate with those who are inconsistent, even if their technical skills are strong. Over time, opportunities follow patterns. The people who can be counted on are given more responsibility. The people who cannot are limited or replaced.

Work ethic grows when students understand that their choices matter beyond the grade. When deadlines mean something. When quality is expected, not optional. When feedback is part of the process, not a judgment of character.

Unlike initiative, which is about stepping forward, work ethic is about staying power. It is the ability to maintain standards day after day, even when motivation fluctuates. Together, initiative and work ethic form a foundation. One moves the work forward. The other sustains it.

When students leave with both, they leave with something employers value deeply: someone who acts and someone who can be relied on to keep acting when it counts.

10. Leadership

Leadership is not a title or a position. It is influence through behavior.

In classrooms, leadership often appears in small, unassigned moments. A student who organizes materials without being asked. One who steps in to help a peer who is struggling. One who stays focused when others lose momentum. These actions shape the tone of the group, even when no one formally recognizes them.

CTE classrooms provide constant opportunities for leadership because work is shared and outcomes are collective. When students take responsibility for the quality of the work, support teammates, and model professionalism, leadership becomes visible. It does not require dominance or authority. It requires steadiness, accountability, and care for the work and the people involved.

In the workplace, employers value leadership at every level. Teams function better when individuals take ownership, communicate clearly, and act in ways that support the group's success. Many early career employees fail because they never learn how to lead themselves or positively influence others.

Leadership also shows up in how students handle mistakes and pressure. Those who remain composed, accept responsibility, and help the team recover earn trust quickly. Employers remember these behaviors because they reduce conflict and increase reliability.

When students understand leadership as action rather than status, more of them step into it. They learn that leadership is practiced daily through choices, not granted later through promotion. That understanding prepares them to contribute meaningfully wherever they land.

Bringing It Together

These ten skills are not separate silos. They overlap, reinforce each other, and develop through repeated practice. When students manage their time well, communication improves. When professionalism increases, teamwork strengthens. When initiative grows, leadership follows.

The real shift happens when these skills are treated as part of the work, not add-ons. When expectations are clear, behaviors are named, and feedback is consistent, students begin to understand what employers actually mean by "being ready."

In the next chapter, we'll focus on how to build a classroom culture that supports these skills daily, so they are reinforced naturally instead of enforced constantly.

Chapter 4

Culture Is the Curriculum

If employability skills are the destination, classroom culture is the road that gets students there.

That matters because most of the skills employers complain about are not content gaps. They're habit gaps. You can't fix habits with a single lesson, a poster on the wall, or a rubric you print once and forget. Habits are shaped by what gets practiced every day, what gets corrected every day, and what gets tolerated every day.

That's culture. And whether you intended to or not, your classroom already has one.

The uncomfortable part is this: culture forms fast. Students walk in and start testing the environment. How late can I be before it matters? How sloppy can I be before someone calls it out? How much can I get away with on my phone? What happens if I blow off my partner in a group project? What happens if I snap back when I'm corrected?

They do not learn those answers from your syllabus. They learn them from what you do when it happens.

If you want a quick read on your culture, don't look at the lesson plan. Look at four moments that happen in every CTE classroom.

What happens when a student shows up late?

What happens when a group member doesn't pull their weight?

What happens when someone makes a mistake and gets frustrated?

What happens when a guest speaker or employer walks in?

Those moments tell the truth. They reveal what your classroom values, what it excuses, and what it trains.

In a classroom with a strong employability culture, students understand something that is easy to say and hard to build: it's not just about completing the task. It's about how you complete the task. They know professional behavior is not something you "turn on" later at the internship. It starts now; in the way they speak, show up, handle feedback, and treat other people.

You've seen the difference. A guest speaker walks into one class and half the room keeps working with earbuds in. Another class stands up, makes eye contact, and one student steps forward to greet them. Same campus. Same age group. Different culture.

That difference rarely comes from charisma. It comes from expectations that were set early and reinforced often.

One of the simplest ways to build that culture is through language. Your words train students how to interpret what's happening. The same correction can feel like punishment or coaching depending on how you frame it.

"Don't be late" sounds like a school rule.

"On the job, being ten minutes early is being on time" sounds like preparation.

"Be quiet" sounds like control.

"Let's practice active listening like you would with a customer or a patient" sounds like professional training.

Those small shifts matter because they connect the classroom to the workplace. Students are more likely to buy into expectations when they understand you're not making up rules to be difficult. You're translating real world standards into a training environment.

But language alone isn't enough. Culture isn't built through a speech. It's built through repetition, which means routines.

Routines take all the mystery out of "soft skills." They make the expected behavior visible. They also reduce the mental load on you because you stop reteaching the same expectations from scratch every period.

You don't need complicated systems. You need a few consistent practices that keep employability skills in the air.

A simple bell ringer can do more than people realize, as long as it isn't fluff. Once a week, ask something that forces reflection on behavior, not just content. What did you do last week that showed leadership? When did you handle feedback well? Where did you lose focus, and what caused it? Those questions start training students to pay attention to how they operate, not just what they produce.

Rotating job roles is another culture builder that feels natural in CTE because it mirrors real work. Safety officer. Timekeeper. Project manager. Quality checker. Cleanup lead. The title matters less than the responsibility. When students carry a role that impacts the whole class, they start to understand accountability in a different way.

I spoke with an Ag Mech teacher, Mr. Tran, who introduced rotating job roles. At first, students rolled their eyes. That part is normal. The second week, something shifted. Students started reminding each other: "That's your job." Not in a tattling way. In a shared expectations way. The teacher didn't have to chase everything. The room began to hold itself to a higher standard.

That is the point. You're not trying to become stricter. You're trying to make expectations communal and automatic.

Modeling matters too, and most teachers underestimate it. Students watch how you respond when you're frustrated, rushed, or wrong. If you want them to learn professionalism, you have to let them see what professionalism looks like under stress.

That might mean narrating your own behavior occasionally. "I messed that up. I own it. I'm going to fix it." That sounds small, but it teaches a bigger lesson: mistakes are normal. Avoiding responsibility is not.

There's one more shift that makes culture building easier and more consistent. Stop seeing behavior as primarily a discipline issue and start seeing it as a career readiness issue.

A student who consistently turns in late work isn't just "unmotivated." They're building a habit that gets people fired. A student who refuses to work with others isn't just being difficult. They're dodging one of the most basic workplace expectations. A student who can't take correction without sarcasm is practicing a response that will cost them opportunities.

That doesn't mean you punish harder. It means you coach more directly.

When you correct behavior, connect it to their future. Would this be acceptable on a jobsite? What would your supervisor do? If this were your internship, what would you change? If your teammate depended on you for safety, would this be good enough?

Those questions land differently than "because I said so." They also reinforce that your classroom is not a generic school space. It's a training ground.

A culinary teacher I met with, Mrs. Hill, told me she used to treat employability skills like an opening week topic. She'd cover professionalism early, move on, and then spend the rest of the year frustrated when students didn't act professional.

Then she changed her approach.

Now, when a student shows up without an apron, she doesn't just talk about dress code. She talks about what the customer sees, what the team depends on, and what the workplace expects. When a student rushes through cleanup, she connects it to sanitation and trust. When a student takes feedback personally, she reframes it as growth.

She told me, "I stopped separating the skills. I just started treating them like part of the work."

That's the move.

Your job is not to create a perfect classroom. Your job is to create an environment where the habits employers need are practiced so often they become normal. When that happens, you spend less time enforcing and more time teaching. Students spend less time guessing what matters and more time rising to the standard.

In the next section of this book, we're going to step out of the classroom for a moment and listen to the workplace directly. Not in vague terms. Through real industry voices. Because once teachers hear what employers are actually saying, it becomes harder to treat these skills as optional and easier to teach them on purpose.

Part II

*What Employers Really Need (and Why
Schools Must Change)*

By the time students reach the end of high school, most of them have spent years being evaluated on what they know. Grades, tests, certifications, and credentials follow them from class to class. On paper, it can look like preparation.

But preparation is not the same thing as readiness.

Readiness shows up when the work gets real. When deadlines matter. When mistakes affect other people. When communication breaks down or when someone has to step forward without being told.

That is where employability skills stop being abstract and start becoming visible.

This section exists because too often we talk about workforce readiness without listening closely to the people who actually hire, train, supervise, and depend on workers every day. Not in theory. Not in policy discussions. In real environments where performance has consequences.

Over the last several years, I have had the opportunity to work alongside employers, business owners, and industry leaders across different sectors. The more I listened, the more a pattern became impossible to ignore. These conversations rarely started with technical skill gaps. They started with behavior. Communication. Reliability. Initiative. The ability to work with others and manage oneself under pressure.

What surprised me was not how often these themes came up. It was how consistent they were across industries that look nothing alike. Construction, healthcare, technology, hospitality. Different tools. Different risks. Different workdays. The expectations, however, were strikingly similar.

This section brings those voices forward.

Not to criticize schools. Not to diminish the importance of technical training. And not to suggest that teachers are doing something wrong. Instead, these chapters make visible what the workplace already assumes. Employability skills are not extra. They are not nice to haves. They are structural.

They shape who gets trusted. Who gets more responsibility. Who advances. And who quietly gets left behind.

As you read the chapters that follow, resist the urge to focus on the details of each industry. The job titles will change. The environments will change. The pressures will change.

What does not change is behavior.

Listen for how often employers talk about communication before competence. About reliability before expertise. About attitude before advancement. Listen for the moments where technical skill was present, but success was not. And for the moments where growth happened because someone showed up ready to learn, ready to listen, and ready to take ownership.

These are not exceptional stories. They are ordinary ones. And that is exactly the point.

This section is not about one model, one company, or one career path. It is about how work actually functions when people depend on one another. The chapters that follow do not argue that schools should change. They simply show why they must.

In the next section, we will turn from employer voices to classroom practice. Not with sweeping reforms or added programs, but with practical ways teachers can build the habits, routines, and expectations that employers already rely on.

Because the goal is not to prepare students for one job.

It is to prepare them to work.

Chapter 5

Student-Led Agency and Career Bridge: When Students Are Treated Like Professionals

Contributing Author Note

Significant portions of this chapter are written by **Eloy Garza**, educator, workforce innovator, and the creator of the Student-Led Agency methodology and the Career Bridge work based learning management system. Garza's contributions draw directly from his experience designing, implementing, and scaling this model across high school Career and Technical Education programs, community colleges, and universities. His voice is intentionally preserved in this chapter to document the origins, evolution, and application of the work in his own words.

Why Authentic Responsibility Changes Everything

Ask employers what separates new hires who grow quickly from those who stall, and the answer is rarely surprising. It is not technical skill. It is everything else. Communication. Initiative.

Accountability. Judgment in situations that are not scripted. The ability to manage yourself, work with others, and follow through when there is no clear path or checklist.

These skills are not extras that sit on top of content. They are the conditions under which content becomes usable.

And yet, most learning environments do not require students to practice those conditions in any sustained or consequential way. Students complete assignments, earn grades, and move on. Even well designed projects often end at the classroom door, with no audience beyond the teacher and no consequences beyond the rubric. Responsibility is simulated. Stakes are artificial. Ownership is limited.

That gap between knowing and functioning is where many capable students stall. It's not a matter of intelligence or effort. It's a lack of environments where their decisions, communication, and follow-through actually matter to someone else.

That is why the Student-Led Agency model stood out to me the first time I encountered it in practice. It did not attempt to teach employability skills as content. It required them as a condition of participation. The model did not ask students to imagine the workplace. It placed them inside it.

What struck me immediately was not the sophistication of the projects or the polish of the student work. It was the way responsibility had been structured. Students were not protected from the discomfort of real expectations. They were coached through it. They were not shielded from consequences. They were supported in learning how to respond to them.

That distinction matters. It is the difference between preparing students to perform and preparing them to function.

How the Student-Led Agency Model Took Shape in Secondary CTE

At this point, it is important to step back and understand where this work began and why it developed the way it did. Eloy Garza, who created the Student-Led Agency methodology and later built the Career Bridge system that supports it, describes the origins this way:

> *Across industries, employers consistently report that the greatest predictors of early career success are not limited to technical competence, but include communication, initiative, accountability, problem solving, collaboration, and professionalism in real work settings. Students rarely develop these habits through isolated projects or classroom simulations. They develop them when they are placed in environments where responsibility is authentic, expectations are clear, and the outcomes of their work matter to people beyond the classroom.*

The Student-Led Agency methodology was created in response to that reality. It originated in secondary Career and Technical Education programs in South Texas, particularly within high school Marketing and Business courses, where students began working directly with small businesses and community organizations on authentic projects. Over time, the methodology expanded across multiple CTE pathways, including Business Management, Audio Video Production, Graphic Design, Photography, Engineering, Accounting, and Finance.

Students did not role play professional engagement. They acted as emerging professionals who were responsible for real deliverables, real communication, and real accountability to external partners. These learning environments positioned students at the highest levels of Bloom's Taxonomy, where they synthesized knowledge, evaluated challenges, and created original solutions for organizations that would actually use their work.

That last point is easy to overlook, but it is central to why the model works. Bloom's Taxonomy is often treated as a planning framework, something teachers reference when designing questions or assessments. In Student-Led Agency environments, Bloom's becomes a lived experience. Students are not asked to analyze or create because a lesson plan requires it. They are required to do so because someone outside the classroom is depending on their work.

The rigor does not come from harder content. It comes from authentic responsibility.

When students are accountable to real clients, cognitive demand increases naturally. They must evaluate competing priorities, revise work based on feedback, justify decisions, and communicate clearly across roles and personalities. These are not academic exercises. They are professional behaviors developed through use.

What began in high school Marketing and Business courses did not remain isolated there. As educators saw the impact on student confidence, communication, and ownership, the methodology expanded into additional pathways. The content changed, but the expectations did not. Whether students were producing marketing assets, engineering solutions, or financial analyses, they were expected to function as contributors to real work rather than participants in simulated assignments.

This is where the distinction between activity and agency becomes clear. Students were not simply busy. They were responsible.

When Success Creates a New Problem and Career Bridge Becomes Necessary

As Student-Led Agency spread from a few classrooms to entire campuses, a predictable pressure point showed up. The approach was working, but real world projects at scale exposed the systems you have to build to keep the work authentic.

Eloy describes that turning point candidly:

> *As the model gained traction across campuses and districts, a new challenge emerged. The instructional methodology was producing strong outcomes, but the scale and complexity of authentic work based learning demanded structure. Teachers needed a way to manage milestones, track student hours and engagement, document artifacts and portfolios, align outcomes to competencies, and collect feedback from students, faculty, and employers.*
>
> *Career Bridge was designed to meet that need as a Work-Based Learning Management System that supports, organizes, and documents environments like the Student-Led Agency methodology. The methodology creates the conditions of authentic professional responsibility. The system provides the infrastructure that allows those conditions to operate consistently across programs, teachers, classrooms, and institutions.*

This is an important distinction, and it is one that often gets blurred in conversations about innovation. Student-Led Agency is the instructional model. It defines how learning happens. Career Bridge is the system that makes that learning sustainable, visible, and scalable.

Without structure, authentic work based learning becomes fragile. It relies heavily on individual teachers managing relationships, tracking progress, documenting learning, and holding students accountable, all while maintaining instructional coherence. That level of complexity is difficult to sustain, especially as programs grow or expand across institutions.

Career Bridge emerged not as a replacement for the learning environment, but as a response to its success. It organizes projects into milestone based workflows. It captures student artifacts and portfolios. It supports employer and faculty feedback. It integrates reflection directly into the work process rather than treating it as an add-on.

As Eloy puts it, the pedagogy drives the learning experience. The system sustains and measures it.

This combination allowed the model to move beyond individual classrooms. Career Bridge was first implemented to support secondary CTE programs in the Rio Grande Valley. As participating students transitioned into higher education, institutions recognized that the same structure could help bridge gaps between academic coursework and professional expectations.

What changed was not the philosophy. What changed was the scale.

From Secondary Classrooms to Postsecondary Learning Environments

Once the Student-Led Agency methodology was established in secondary CTE classrooms, its expansion into postsecondary environments was not a shift in philosophy so much as a test of durability. The question was not whether the model worked with older students, but whether it could maintain its integrity across larger institutions, broader disciplines, and more complex partnerships. Eloy describes that transition as both natural and revealing:

> *Career Bridge was first implemented to support secondary CTE programs in the Rio Grande Valley. As participating students transitioned into higher education, institutions recognized that the same model could help bridge gaps between academic coursework and professional expectations. The methodology and platform then expanded into community college programs and later into university courses, including large-scale implementation at the University of Texas Rio Grande Valley.*
>
> *Students across disciplines engaged in applied projects that connected theory with real world problem solving for employers and community organizations, with Career Bridge serving as the system that aligned milestones, assessment, reflection, and partner engagement.*

What is important here is what did not change. Students were still expected to function as contributors rather than participants. Faculty still served as instructional and professional mentors rather than managers of simulated tasks. Employers and community partners remained collaborators with real expectations, not guest speakers or symbolic audiences.

What did change was scope. Projects became more complex. Teams became more interdisciplinary. Timelines extended. The work carried higher stakes, because outcomes were visible beyond the classroom.

The same habits that had helped high school students develop confidence and professionalism translated directly into postsecondary contexts. Communication still mattered. Follow through still mattered. Initiative still mattered. The difference was that students now had to manage those expectations while balancing increased academic demands, employment, and personal responsibilities.

The model did not soften under pressure. It sharpened.

That durability is what allowed the work to expand beyond a single institution. As Eloy notes, the methodology and system eventually extended into Chicago based university initiatives, where students engaged in technology audits, operational improvement projects, consulting work, and social impact initiatives. The settings were different. The expectations were the same.

Across all of these contexts, Career Bridge provided a shared structure that made the learning visible, documentable, and transferable. The system did not replace teaching. It supported it by ensuring continuity, accountability, and reflection at scale.

Entering the Work as a Client Through the RGV LEAD Innovation Hub

My experience with this model did not begin as an observer or evaluator. I entered it as a client.

I did not join because I was looking for interns. I joined after seeing a post from RGV LEAD inviting small businesses to partner with UTRGV student teams through the RGV LEAD Innovation Hub. The program was positioned clearly. In partnership with UTRGV Marketing faculty and powered by Career Bridge, student teams would provide structured, faculty guided support to local businesses at a cost that made participation accessible.

The invitation aligned with RGV LEAD's long-standing mission of connecting education and industry, and I was interested in supporting that work while potentially gaining insight for Beacon Administrative Consulting. I paid the enrollment fee and went in with reasonable expectations. A marketing plan. Some usable materials. A solid experience.

I underestimated the model.

From the first meeting, it was clear that these students were not being treated as a class completing an assignment. They were being treated as a firm with a client, a scope of work, and an obligation to deliver. Their nervousness was visible, but so was their ownership. They were not waiting to be told what to say. They were listening carefully, asking clarifying questions, and documenting next steps. Week by week, I watched the shift take place. Students improved not because they were told to revise, but because the work demanded it. Communication became clearer. Questions became more precise. Follow ups became more consistent. They learned to manage progress, not just produce artifacts.

I also chose to open the door to the realities of running a consulting business. Services, pricing, growth plans, and the challenges behind the scenes were all on the table. I did not simplify the work for them. I trusted them with it.

They responded the way professionals do when they are trusted with real information. They wanted to contribute. They wanted to understand the why behind decisions. They adjusted when feedback required it.

One student, Ruth, stood out early. She took initiative without being prompted. She followed up consistently. She proposed solutions and adapted when feedback changed direction. Her presence raised the pace of the group.

If Beacon were hiring today, she would be on my shortlist.

That experience reinforced something I had believed for years but had rarely seen executed so intentionally. Students rise to the level of responsibility we are willing to trust them with when the environment supports that trust.

The Student View From Inside the Work

Ruth later reflected on what the experience required of her, and her perspective captures the difference between simulated learning and authentic responsibility more clearly than any framework could.

She described how working with a real client forced her to strengthen communication, both externally and within her team. She spoke honestly about navigating a group where she could not choose her teammates and where expectations had to be communicated clearly in order to succeed. As the only marketing major on the team, she felt pressure, but she also learned that naming concerns early and setting expectations directly made collaboration stronger rather than more difficult.

Time management became real when deliverables had consequences. Milestone reports were not busywork. They were anchors that kept the team moving forward even while balancing other classes, work, and responsibilities.

More importantly, Ruth recognized things about herself that classroom simulations had never revealed. She acknowledged gaps in her presentation and communication skills. She admitted to taking on too much responsibility instead of asking for support. Balancing life as a mother, student, and full-time employee forced her to prioritize, seek feedback, and adjust how she worked with others.

Her reflection on employability skills was not abstract. It was practical. Customer service experience had already taught her that technical knowledge alone does not carry a team. The Student-Led Agency environment, supported by Career Bridge, gave her a place to practice those lessons in a professional setting, where communication, teamwork, and initiative were not optional and where growth was visible.

That is what authentic learning sounds like.

Students do not talk about grades. They talk about expectations, pressure, feedback, and responsibility. They talk about learning how to function, not just how to perform.

And that distinction is the heart of this work.

Why the Model Works When Others Stall

Structure, Not Motivation

By the time most educators encounter a model like Student-Led Agency supported by Career Bridge, the question is no longer whether students are capable. The question is why this works when so many well-intentioned strategies do not.

The answer is not energy, novelty, or motivation. It is structure.

Most classrooms ask students to behave professionally without placing them inside environments that require professionalism. Expectations are stated, sometimes modeled, but rarely enforced by the work itself. When consequences are abstract or delayed, behaviors remain optional.

This model removes that gap.

As Eloy explains, accountability does not have to be imposed when it is embedded:

> *From the perspective of participating employers and partners, the distinction between simulated coursework and authentic engagement was immediately visible. Students learned to manage ambiguity, communicate expectations, accept feedback, and assume ownership of outcomes. They did not perform for grades alone. They performed for clients and communities.*
>
> *The Career Bridge WBLMS ensured that this work was structured, guided, and documented so that learning was not only experienced, but also measurable.*

This is the critical shift. Professional behaviors are no longer discussed as ideals. They are required for progress. Communication determines whether work moves forward or stalls. Initiative determines whether problems are addressed or ignored. Time management determines whether commitments are met or missed.

The instructor's role changes as well. Eloy has said repeatedly that the goal is not to remove support, but to reposition it. Faculty do not disappear. They coach. They observe. They intervene when necessary. But they do not rescue students from the consequences of their own communication, planning, or follow through.

That distinction matters.

When accountability moves from imposed to owned, employability skills stop being theoretical. They become survival tools. Students do not ask what the minimum is. They ask what good work looks like.

That shift is the outcome.

What This Teaches Us About Employability Skills at Every Level

Although Career Bridge operates most visibly at the postsecondary level, its implications extend far beyond colleges and universities. The principles underlying the Student-Led Agency methodology apply anywhere students are learning how to work.

Middle school programs. High school pathways. CTE classrooms. Any environment where real responsibility can be introduced in developmentally appropriate ways.

What matters is not the platform. It is the mindset.

Deadlines matter when someone is depending on the work. Communication matters when misunderstanding has consequences.

Professionalism matters when behavior represents the student to someone outside the classroom.

This is not curriculum. It is culture.

Eloy makes this point directly:

> *The transition from secondary to postsecondary settings did not require a change in philosophy. The same practices that helped high school students develop confidence and professionalism also prepared university students to function effectively in multidisciplinary teams serving real clients. What changed was the scale, scope, and geographic reach of projects.*

That observation should challenge a common assumption in education. We often treat employability skills as something students will develop later, once they are older, more mature, or closer to graduation. The evidence here suggests the opposite. When students are trusted earlier with meaningful work, coached intentionally, and supported by clear systems, they grow into the expectations placed on them.

Waiting does not prepare students. Structure does.

This is why the work you have seen throughout this book does not require a wholesale redesign of your classroom. The same habits that power Student-Led Agency show up in daily routines. Clear expectations. Observable behaviors. Reflection tied to real work. Feedback that mirrors professional language rather than academic judgment.

Career Bridge makes those elements visible at scale. Classrooms can do the same thing on a smaller canvas.

One of the most important contributions of this model is that it refuses to separate education from workforce reality. It does not treat employability skills as a soft overlay on technical content. It treats them as structural conditions.

As Eloy summarizes:

> *The result is a system in which technical knowledge and durable employability skills develop together. The Student-Led Agency methodology provides the learning environment. Career Bridge ensures continuity, accountability, and scalability across programs and institutions. Together, they create a bridge between secondary and postsecondary education, between coursework and career environments, and between individual student effort and regional workforce development priorities.*

That bridge matters because it aligns what educators teach with what employers actually experience. Across industries, employers say the same thing in different words. Technical skills open the door. Employability skills determine who lasts.

After seeing this model in action, I knew it could not stand alone as an isolated example. I wanted to test its lessons across construction, healthcare, technology, and hospitality. Different pressures. Different risks. Same expectations.

That is why the next chapter turns directly to employer voices. Their perspectives reinforce what Student-Led Agency and Career Bridge make visible. These skills are not optional. They are not contextual. They are foundational.

And when we build environments that require them, students are capable of far more than we often assume.

Chapter 6

Building More Than Structures: What Bechtel Taught Me About Employability

If you have never stood near a large construction site, it is difficult to understand the scale of what is happening. The noise never stops. People move with purpose in every direction. Equipment, materials, schedules, and safety protocols all have to line up perfectly for progress to happen. It feels less like a jobsite and more like a living system.

I was reminded of that when I spoke with Patrick, a workforce development specialist with Bechtel. His team is involved in building one of the largest LNG plants in the world, right here in South Texas. When most people think about a project like that, they picture steel, cranes, and engineering marvels.

Patrick talked about people.

Thousands of them.

On a single site, there can be three to five thousand workers at a time. Electricians. Pipefitters. Instrument technicians. Safety teams.

Inspectors. Project managers. Support staff. People from across the country and, in many cases, from across the world. These projects last for years. Some stretch five, seven, even ten years before the final work is complete.

That kind of environment exposes something important. It shows very quickly what it actually takes to succeed in a workplace. Not just in construction, but anywhere.

Patrick has trained, evaluated, and worked alongside hundreds of employees over the years. As he talked, a pattern became clear. The people who advance are not always the most technically gifted. They are the ones others can rely on.

That is the real lesson of this chapter.

Trust Is the Currency

When I asked Patrick how apprentices are selected for Bechtel's workforce development programs, I expected him to talk about certifications or test scores. Instead, he said something simple and direct.

Superintendents choose the people they trust.

Trust determines opportunity.

That trust is not built on raw talent alone. It comes from consistency. From communication. From how someone responds when things do not go as planned. In an environment where a single miscommunication can cause injury, delay a project, or cost millions of dollars, these habits matter more than most people realize.

Patrick described the workers who earn that trust. They show up every day. They communicate early instead of waiting for problems to grow. They ask questions when they are unsure. They offer help without being asked. They carry themselves professionally. They stay composed under pressure. They do not bring unnecessary drama to the jobsite.

None of that sounds complicated. But in a workforce of thousands, it makes all the difference.

As Patrick put it, technical skills can be taught. Attitude, work ethic, communication, and humility are much harder to build once someone enters the workforce without them.

Two Workers, Two Paths

Patrick shared a story that has stayed with me.

Years ago, he worked with a pipefitter who was extraordinarily skilled. This worker completed a multi-hour certification exam in thirty minutes and earned a perfect score. His technical ability was undeniable. He could do things with pipe that few others could match.

But his career stalled.

Poor communication, inconsistent attitude, and difficulty working with others limited his growth. He had the skill to lead, but not the habits people look for in leaders. Over time, opportunities went to others.

Then Patrick described another worker. This one entered the field with limited technical experience, but with humility and a strong desire to learn. He listened carefully. He communicated clearly. He owned mistakes. He welcomed feedback. He sought guidance from experienced workers instead of pretending he knew everything.

That worker advanced steadily. Eventually, he left construction and became the lead instrumentation technician at a chemical plant. Same jobsite. Same expectations. Very different outcomes.

Success followed the person who built trust, not just the person who demonstrated competence.

A Message Students Rarely Hear

When I asked Patrick what he would tell a high school student considering a career in construction or the trades, he did not sugar-coat it. The work is hard. It is hot. You will go home tired.

Then he said something every student deserves to hear.

You can build a life doing this work. You can support a family, buy a home, and build stability. You just have to be someone others can count on.

He also pushed back on a message students hear far too often. College is not the only path. Education is. Learning happens in

70

many forms. Apprenticeships. Certifications. On the job training. Mentorship. CTE pathways.

Students who are willing to learn, ask questions, take feedback, and practice consistently can build strong careers without ever stepping onto a university campus. Many already do.

But the students who succeed are the ones who know how to show up. On time. Prepared. Willing to communicate instead of hiding confusion. Ready to learn from mistakes.

The trades are not for everyone. But they are a powerful option for students who want their work to matter and who take pride in building something real.

What Teachers Shape Every Day

When our conversation turned to teachers, Patrick focused on something that surprised me. He said the greatest gift teachers can give students today is patience.

Many students do not grow up using tools at home. They are not exposed to mechanical systems the way previous generations were. Cars are computers now. Products are replaced instead of repaired. Expecting students to walk into a CTE classroom with foundational skills their grandparents learned early in life is unrealistic.

Patrick described the approach that works. Show the task. Let students try. Let them fail. Then help them analyze what happened. He referred to these moments as lessons learned, not failures.

Struggle is part of learning.

He also emphasized communication. Many young workers struggle because they have never practiced professional communication. They do not know the difference between talking to friends and speaking to supervisors. Between venting frustration and reporting a problem clearly. Between casual language and professional tone. That is where classrooms matter.

Every group project becomes practice for teamwork. Every deadline becomes practice for accountability. Every presentation becomes practice for workplace communication. Every conflict becomes a chance to practice problem solving.

Teachers are not just teaching content. They are shaping how students' function in environments where others depend on them.

The Academic Skills That Matter More Than Students Think

When I asked Patrick about technical preparation, he did not dismiss safety or blueprint reading. But he emphasized two foundational skills students often underestimate.

Reading and math.

Not abstract versions, but applied ones.

Reading blueprints requires strong comprehension and spatial reasoning. Measuring and fabrication rely on fractions, geometry, and trigonometry. Pipefitters use the Pythagorean Theorem regularly, whether they realize it or not.

When students say they will never use this in real life, they are often wrong. Especially if they want a career that pays well.

The connection between academics and the workplace is direct. When we fail to make that connection visible, students miss opportunities they might otherwise embrace.

The Lesson That Carries Across Industries

After spending time with Patrick, the lesson that stayed with me had nothing to do with construction schedules or project size.

Careers are not separated by technical skill alone. They are separated by employability.

The ability to communicate clearly. To work respectfully. To manage yourself. To keep learning. To stay steady under pressure. To take initiative. To carry yourself professionally even when no one is watching.

We often call these soft skills, but there is nothing soft about them. They are the backbone of employability. They shape trust. They determine growth. They influence leadership.

Technical skills matter. But employability skills determine whether those technical skills actually lead somewhere.

After that conversation, I wanted to know whether the same patterns held true in other fields. So I spoke with leaders in healthcare, information technology, and hospitality.

The environments could not be more different.

Their answers were nearly identical.

We are not preparing students for one job.

We are preparing them for every job.

The next chapter brings their voices into the conversation.

Chapter 7

What Employers Really See: Voices from Healthcare, IT, and Hospitality

Teachers often ask me whether employability skills really matter as much as employers say they do. Not in theory, but in practice. In the real places where real people earn real paychecks.

After finishing my interviews with leaders from the construction industry, conversations that made the importance of soft skills unmistakably clear, I wanted to test the pattern in other sectors. So I reached out to three people who work far from construction, in completely different environments with completely different expectations: a nurse practitioner in a high stakes clinical setting, an IT manager for a major telecommunications company, and a manager for one of South Padre Island's busiest vacation rental and property management operations.

These industries don't look alike in any meaningful way. One deals with patient lives, one with mission critical technology, and one with customers whose expectations shift by the hour. But when you listen closely, their expectations for employees are not just similar, they are nearly identical.

What follows is a look inside their world. What they see. What they value. What frustrates them. And above all, what they wish young people understood before stepping into the workforce.

Because if there's one thing these employers made clear, it's this: Technical skills might get you hired. Employability skills determine whether you succeed.

Healthcare: Clarity, Composure, and Communication

Theresa, a nurse practitioner who began her career in bedside nursing before moving to the ICU and eventually earning her NP credential, works in an environment where mistakes carry consequences measured in heartbeats. Her world demands precision, confidence, and calm under pressure, but just as much, it demands communication.

When I asked what separates nurses who thrive from those who struggle, she didn't hesitate. "Time management," she said. "Communication. Initiative." Skills that don't show up on a patient chart but reveal themselves in every minute of the day.

She described new nurses who enter the field academically prepared but practically overwhelmed. They can recite textbook information, but they struggle to organize their shift, anticipate problems, or communicate clearly with physicians, therapists, and families. "Closed loop communication," the simple discipline of confirming an instruction by repeating it back, makes an enormous difference. It prevents errors long before they reach the bedside, and yet many new healthcare workers have never practiced it in school. Theresa also talked about the behaviors that quietly sabotage promising new professionals. Showing up with complaints but no solutions. Failing to communicate changes in patient conditions. Delivering messages in ways that escalate tension instead of building teamwork. "We can teach the technical pieces," she told me. "We can teach procedures. But communication, that's what makes or breaks you."

And yet, she also shared story after story of early career nurses who grew rapidly because they possessed something deeper: a willingness to ask questions, an ability to stay composed when things got chaotic, and the humility to accept feedback without defensiveness. Those nurses weren't perfect, she said. They were teachable. And teachability is a soft skill too.

Information Technology: Problem Solving and the Willingness to Learn

If healthcare rewards composure, IT rewards curiosity. Chris, an IT manager for an internet service provider, started his career in technical support. What moved him upward wasn't extraordinary technical knowledge, it was the decision to raise his hand.

Anytime a project needed help, he volunteered. He didn't always know what to do, but he was willing to figure it out. That willingness alone changed the trajectory of his career.

"The best IT people aren't the ones who know everything," he said. "They're the ones who know how to break a problem apart and communicate what they're seeing." He told me about new employees who crumble when they encounter something unfamiliar, and others who stay curious, calm, and proactive. The difference, again, is not technical skill, it's mindset.

Chris has supervised employees with tremendous technical talent who could repair anything but couldn't collaborate, couldn't communicate, and refused to share knowledge. Those employees rarely lasted. In contrast, he described one employee who came from the billing department, not IT. What made her successful was her communication, her initiative, and her ability to translate technical instructions into plain language for customers and internal teams. She lacked the classic technical background, and ended up outpacing people who had it.

When I asked what schools could do better, his answer sounded almost like a transcript from Theresa: teach students how to think, how to communicate, and how to manage their own learning. Even math, often treated as an abstract hurdle, showed up again as a training ground for problem solving. IT doesn't require calculus, he said, but it absolutely requires the mindset that math develops:

breaking things into pieces, analyzing patterns, and evaluating solutions.

Hospitality and Property Management: Communication, Initiative, and Adaptability

Matthew works in a completely different universe, hospitality and property management on South Padre Island. His company oversees every part of the experience: reservations, guest communication, maintenance, housekeeping, and emergency response when something unexpected goes wrong, which can happen anytime.

What surprised me most was how closely his list of essential skills matched those from healthcare and IT. In his world, initiative is everything. Employees who wait for instructions fall behind. Employees who anticipate needs, step forward, and solve problems rise quickly.

He explained how customer expectations shift rapidly, sometimes hourly. People who can adapt, think, communicate clearly, and keep their composure outperform those who freeze under pressure, even when the latter have more experience. "Young employees who are willing to learn the whole business," he said, "not just their department, grow the fastest."

Matthew described standout employees who transformed their roles not by technical expertise but through clear communication and a willingness to take ownership. He also shared stories of highly skilled maintenance workers who frustrated customers because they failed to explain what they were doing or didn't follow through. Talent wasn't the problem, communication was.

And, echoing the others, he emphasized how rare it is to find young adults who are comfortable speaking face to face. Too many default to texting, even for high stakes communication. "They're not bad at communicating," he said. "They just haven't practiced."

Three Industries, One Message

When you place these interviews side by side, a pattern emerges so consistent it's impossible to ignore. These employers don't know one another. They don't share a field, a vocabulary, or even similar work environments. Yet they are living the same reality.

Communication matters more than credentials.

Problem solving matters more than procedures.

Initiative matters more than experience.

Adaptability matters more than technical mastery.

Professionalism matters everywhere.

Technical skills open doors. Employability skills determine whether someone walks through, and whether they're invited to stay.

Across every conversation, I heard echoes of the same idea: "We can teach the technical work. What we need are people who can communicate, collaborate, stay calm, think clearly, and keep going when things get difficult."

A Message to Teachers

This chapter is not simply a reminder of the importance of soft skills. It is evidence, straight from the people who supervise, train, and evaluate employees every day.

Our students need technical competency, yes. But they also need something schools too often assume they'll acquire on their own. The ability to talk to people. The confidence to solve problems without panicking. The discipline to manage time and follow through. The humility to ask questions. The professionalism to represent themselves, and their future companies, with respect.

These are not extras. They are essentials. They determine whether a young person becomes an asset or a liability. Whether they rise or stall. Whether they thrive or burn out.

And the good news is this: these skills can be taught. They can be practiced. They can be embedded in every classroom, every pathway, every project.

Looking Ahead

Having heard from construction, healthcare, IT, and hospitality, one truth has become unmistakable. We are not preparing students for one job. We are preparing them for every job.

The employability skills in this book are not tied to an industry. They are tied to human nature and workplace culture.

In the next chapter, we step back from these voices and translate their insights into practical tools teachers can implement immediately, no matter what they teach, who their students are, or where their graduates will work.

Because every employer is telling us the same thing.

And our students deserve to hear it too.

Part III

Practical Strategies for the Classroom

Up to this point, we have talked about why employability skills matter, what employers actually expect, and how those expectations show up across industries. None of that is theoretical. It is grounded in real classrooms, real worksites, and real consequences for students once they graduate.

The question now is a practical one.

What does this look like on Monday morning?

Part III is about application. It is about turning expectations into habits and habits into culture, without adding another initiative or overwhelming an already full plate. The strategies in this section are designed for real classrooms, taught by real CTE teachers, under real constraints. They are not packaged programs or scripted lessons. They are adjustments, routines, and instructional choices that build employability skills alongside technical instruction.

This section focuses on what can be embedded, not added. Bell ringers that shape mindset. Routines that reinforce professionalism. Projects that require collaboration and accountability. Feedback that coach's behavior instead of just scoring it. Assessment practices that help students understand where they are and how to grow. You will not find a one size fits all model here. What you will find are examples, structures, and questions that help you adapt these ideas to your pathway, your students, and you're setting. Whether you teach welding, health science, culinary arts, business, or agriculture, the underlying behaviors employers expect are remarkably consistent.

The chapters that follow are meant to be used, not admired. Some strategies will fit your classroom immediately. Others may spark ideas you modify over time. The goal is not to implement everything at once, but to be intentional about how employability skills show up in daily instruction.

When these skills are reinforced consistently, they stop feeling like a separate focus. They become part of how students work, interact, and take responsibility for their learning. That is where preparation becomes durable, and where technical skills begin to carry real weight beyond the classroom.

Chapter 8

Daily Strategies That Work

You do not need a new curriculum, a new course, or a separate unit to teach employability skills. In fact, the more we isolate these skills, the less likely students are to use them when it counts.

What students need instead is repetition. Context. Feedback. And permission to practice these behaviors in low stakes ways before the stakes get high.

If you have ever taught students to clean a workstation before leaving, run a safety check before starting a task, or prepare for a customer or guest, you are already teaching employability. You just may not have been calling it that.

The difference between "hoping students pick it up" and actually building the skill is intention. Naming the behavior. Reinforcing it. Connecting it to work beyond the classroom.

This chapter focuses on daily strategies that fit inside the class you already teach. These are not add-ons. They are small routines that quietly shape habits over time.

Bell Ringers That Build Professional Thinking

The first few minutes of class matter more than we often realize. They set the tone. They signal expectations. They tell students what kind of thinking is valued in the room.

Bell ringers do not have to review content to be effective. They can also train students to reflect, communicate, and think like professionals.

A three to five minute prompt at the start of class can keep employability skills visible without feeling forced. Over time, students begin to internalize the language and expectations that employers use every day.

Here are examples you can use immediately:

- How did you show professionalism yesterday, either in this class or somewhere else?
- Describe a time you disagreed with a teammate. How did you handle it?
- What is one employability skill you want to improve this week, and what will you do differently?
- You are the supervisor. What would you do if a team member kept showing up late?
- Think of the best boss, coach, or teacher you have had. What behaviors made them effective?

The goal is not perfect answers. The goal is practice. Writing clearly. Thinking honestly. Connecting behavior to outcomes.

One reason bell ringers work so well is that they lower the stakes. Students aren't being graded on perfection. They're practicing language and thinking they'll need later. Over time, those short moments build a shared vocabulary around professionalism that teachers don't have to reteach from scratch every semester.

A simple move that pays off later is having students keep these responses in a journal or shared digital document. Over time, they build a record of growth. Those same responses can later be used for mock interviews, resume writing, or employer visits.

Practical move: Start a personal bell ringer bank. Build a list of twenty to thirty prompts and rotate them. Consistency matters more than novelty.

Job Roles That Teach Accountability

Group work alone does not teach teamwork. Without structure, it often teaches avoidance, frustration, or task dumping.

Assigning clear roles gives students a reason to take responsibility and a framework for practicing real workplace behaviors. These roles should rotate so every student experiences leadership, support, and accountability.

Common roles that work across pathways include:

- Project Manager, responsible for pacing and follow through
- Quality Checker, responsible for standards and accuracy
- Safety Officer, responsible for protocols and risk awareness

- Presenter or Spokesperson, responsible for communication

The real learning happens in how students grow into these roles. Pay attention to how they handle peer feedback. Notice whether they delegate or simply assign work. Watch how they manage time when no one is hovering.

You do not need elaborate materials to make this work. Simple role cards or badges are enough. What matters is consistency and follow up.

When students begin reminding one another of expectations, you know culture is forming.

From a curriculum standpoint, roles solve problem teachers already know well. Group work often hides effort. Clear roles make contribution visible. That makes feedback fairer, reduces frustration, and gives students a clearer sense of what responsibility actually looks like in a work setting.

Exit Tickets That Measure More Than Content

Most exit tickets check understanding. That matters, but it only tells part of the story.

Exit tickets can also help students reflect on how they showed up, not just what they completed. These reflections build self-awareness, one of the most overlooked employability skills.

Try ending class with questions like:

- What skill did you use today that you will need on the job?

- How did your team work today? What helped or hurt?
- Did you communicate clearly when something went wrong?
- If today were a work shift, how would your supervisor describe your performance?

Patterns emerge quickly. You see who is honest, who avoids accountability, who is learning to reflect, and who is beginning to lead.

One business instructor I worked with used the same three exit questions every week: What did I do well today? What could I improve? How does this connect to work? She told me the change in student self-awareness was immediate.

A simple weekly self-check grid can also help. Students rate themselves on collaboration, communication, initiative, and reliability. These check-ins open the door to meaningful conversations rather than discipline-focused ones.

Building Employability Into What You Already Teach

You do not need a separate lesson to teach employability skills. You can layer them into labs, simulations, and projects that already exist.

Before a task, frame expectations:

What will initiative look like today?

How will you communicate if something goes wrong?

During the task, coach in real time. Walk the room. Name behaviors out loud. When a student steps in to help without being asked, say it. When a team adjusts after feedback, point it out.

After the task, reflect together. Ask what worked. Ask what did not. Ask how an employer would have viewed the work.

This kind of narration helps students connect behavior to outcomes. It turns everyday moments into learning opportunities.

What a Soft Skills–Integrated Day Can Look Like

A class period does not need to feel different to be doing different work.

A typical day might include a reflective bell ringer focused on professionalism, structured group roles during a project, active coaching during independent or lab work, and a short reflection at the end focused on accountability and communication.

You do not have to hit every skill every day. What matters is repetition. Naming the skills. Modeling them. Reinforcing them.

That is how habits form.

What matters most here is not which routine you choose. It's that students encounter these expectations repeatedly and in different contexts. When employability skills show up in warm-ups, projects, labs, and reflections, students stop seeing them as add-ons and start treating them as part of the job.

A Teacher's Perspective

A welding teacher I worked with once told me that the biggest shift came when he stopped treating soft skills as something separate. Once he began asking bell ringer questions about teamwork and professionalism, students started naming those behaviors themselves. One student told him, "I was the safety role yesterday, so I made sure we didn't leave a mess."

Nothing about the class changed structurally. The meaning changed.

That is the point.

Why This Works

These strategies work for one simple reason: they make expectations visible and repeatable.

Students don't develop employability skills from a single lesson or a well-worded rubric. They develop them by encountering the same expectations across different moments. When professionalism shows up in a bell ringer, a group role, a lab activity, and a reflection, it stops feeling optional. It becomes normal.

This approach also respects how CTE classrooms actually function. You are already managing safety, equipment, time, and real work. These routines don't compete with that reality. They fit inside it. Instead of adding new content, they shape how existing work gets done.

Over time, students stop asking, "Is this for a grade?" and start asking, "Is this how it would work on the job?" That shift is the goal. When students begin to self-correct and hold each other accountable, the culture starts doing the work for you.

And that's when employability skills stop being something you teach and start becoming something students practice on their own.

Final Thoughts

Start small. Choose one routine and commit to it.

Use the language of work consistently. Let students reflect on their own behavior, not just their grades. Give feedback on how they show up, not just what they produce.

Students do not just need practice.

They need practice with feedback.

That is how employability is built, one ordinary day at a time.

Chapter 9

Assessing What Matters

For many CTE teachers, assessing employability skills is where confidence starts to wobble.

Teaching these skills makes sense. Employers ask for them constantly. You see their absence every day. But grading them can feel uncomfortable. How do you score something like work ethic or professionalism without it feeling subjective? What does an A even represent when the skill is still developing? And how do you balance fairness when students enter your classroom with very different levels of maturity, confidence, and life experience?

Those are not excuses. They are legitimate concerns.

But here is the reality. When employability skills are never measured, they are rarely taken seriously. Students quickly learn what counts and what does not. If behavior, communication, and accountability never show up in feedback or evaluation, they become background noise. Important in theory. Optional in practice.

At the same time, if assessment becomes overly complex or bureaucratic, it stops serving its purpose. Teachers abandon it. Students disengage. The system collapses under its own weight.

So the goal is not to grade employability skills the way you grade a quiz or a certification exam. The goal is to make expectations visible, to track patterns over time, and to coach growth in the same way you would with a technical skill that is still developing.

That shift changes everything.

Clear Rubrics Ground the Conversation

A strong employability skills rubric does not need to be long or clever. It needs to sound like the workplace.

When teachers struggle with assessing soft skills, it is often because the criteria feel disconnected from real expectations. Students sense that immediately. A rubric becomes meaningful when it describes behaviors they recognize and consequences they can imagine.

Take professionalism as an example. In the workplace, professionalism shows up in attendance, preparation, focus, attitude, and follow-through. A simple rubric that describes what those behaviors look like at different levels gives both teachers and students a shared language.

The power of a rubric is not in the score itself. It is in the conversation it allows you to have. Instead of saying, "You need to be more professional," you can point to specific behaviors and say, "Here is where you are right now, and here is what improvement looks like."

Using a three- or four-point scale is usually enough. It allows for growth without turning assessment into paperwork. More importantly, it reinforces the idea that employability skills are developmental. Students are not labeled. They are coached.

Reflection Builds Self-Awareness

One of the most overlooked assessment tools in CTE classrooms is student reflection.

When students are never asked to think about how they show up, they rarely do it on their own. Reflection changes that. It slows students down long enough to notice patterns in their behavior and connect effort to outcomes.

Weekly self-reflection works particularly well. Choosing just a few focus skills at a time keeps the process manageable. When students score themselves and explain their reasoning, something important happens. They begin to internalize the expectations instead of reacting to them.

Over time, these short reflections reveal growth that grades alone cannot capture. They also give your insight into how students see themselves. That matters. A student who consistently underrates their communication skills may need encouragement and confidence building. A student who consistently overrates their teamwork may need more direct feedback.

Either way, reflection becomes a coaching tool instead of a compliance exercise.

Peer Feedback Makes Expectations Real

Employability skills live in relationships. That is why peer feedback is so effective.

When students receive structured feedback from teammates, expectations stop being theoretical. They become social. Students begin to understand how their behavior affects others, not just their grade.

This does not require a complex system. After a group task or project, a few focused prompts are enough to reinforce habits. Asking students to name what a teammate did well and what could improve next time builds both awareness and accountability.

Using the same rubric for peer feedback that you use for teacher feedback strengthens the impact. Students start to recognize the criteria as shared expectations, not personal opinions. Over time, they begin to anticipate feedback and adjust behavior proactively. That is when employability skills start to stick.

Teacher Observation Still Matters

CTE teachers observe employability skills constantly. During labs, projects, simulations, and group work, you see who stays focused, who steps up, who hesitates, and who avoids responsibility.

The difference between informal observation and intentional assessment is visibility.

A simple observation checklist, used occasionally and strategically, helps turn what you already notice into meaningful feedback. It does not need to be used every day. In fact, it is often most effective when used during key activities where behaviors are most visible. These notes give you concrete examples to reference during conferences, progress checks, or parent conversations. They also protect against vague feedback. Instead of saying, "You need to participate more," you can say, "I noticed you waited for direction even when the task was clear. Let's talk about what initiative looks like here." That level of specificity builds trust.

Grading Versus Coaching

Whether employability skills should be graded formally depends on your program and your district. Some schools include them as part of participation or professionalism grades. Others keep them separate and use them for feedback only.

What matters most is clarity of purpose.

If employability skill assessment becomes punitive, it loses its power. Students shut down. Growth stalls. But when assessment is framed as coaching, students lean in.

The message should always be the same. This is where you are. This is what growth looks like. Here is how you move forward.

That approach mirrors the workplace. Employees are rarely fired for one mistake. They struggle when patterns go unaddressed or when feedback comes too late. Teaching students to respond to feedback now prepares them for those realities later.

Voices From the Field

One health science instructor described how this shift changed her classroom. She explained that once she replaced grading language with coaching language, students stopped arguing about points and started asking about improvement. They wanted to know what better looked like and how to get there. That conversation never happened before.

Employers echo the same sentiment. At a regional workforce discussion, a plant manager said plainly that he can train skills, but he cannot train attitude or accountability. Students who never practice those behaviors in school learn the lesson on the job, often at a much higher cost.

Assessment as Preparation

Assessing employability skills is not about perfection. It is about preparation.

When students know what is expected, see examples of growth, and receive consistent feedback, they begin to take ownership of their behavior. They stop seeing professionalism as a personality trait and start seeing it as a skill they can develop.

That is the goal.

In the next chapter, we will turn our attention to students who struggle most with these expectations. Not to lower the bar, but to support growth in ways that are firm, fair, and realistic.

Chapter 10

Supporting Struggling Students

Every CTE teacher knows this already, even if we do not always say it out loud.

Not every student walks into your classroom ready to behave like a professional. Some are still learning how to manage frustration. Some have never seen adults' model calm communication or accountability. Others have lived through instability, trauma, or chaos and have developed habits that helped them survive, even if those habits do not translate well to the workplace.

That does not make them lazy. It makes them unfinished.

The challenge is that the workplace does not pause for unfinished skills. Employers still expect reliability, communication, and professionalism, regardless of a student's background. That tension is real, and it lands squarely in CTE classrooms.

The good news is that CTE classrooms are often the first place students feel a sense of purpose. They are working with their hands, solving real problems, and seeing a reason to show up. That gives you leverage. And when it is used intentionally, it can help students bridge the gap between where they are and where they need to be.

Coaching Instead of Constant Correction

When a student shows up late again, shuts down during group work, or reacts emotionally to feedback, the instinct is often to default to discipline. Expectations matter. Boundaries matter. Structure matters.

But employability skills do not grow through consequences alone. They grow through coaching.

Several experienced CTE teachers have told me the same thing in different ways. When they stopped treating behavior as a rule violation and started treating it like performance feedback, students listened differently. The conversation shifted from control to growth. That does not mean ignoring behavior. It means reframing the moment. Instead of asking why a student keeps making the same mistake, it helps to ask how that behavior would be interpreted in the workplace. Instead of shutting down frustration, it helps to model what professional problem solving looks like under pressure. This approach does not lower the bar. It shows students how to reach it.

Breaking Soft Skills Into Teachable Parts

One of the biggest mistakes schools make with employability skills is treating them as personality traits instead of skills that can be developed.

If a student struggles with a technical concept, you break it down. You model it. You give them time to practice. You offer feedback. The same approach applies to soft skills.

Professionalism is not one thing. It is a collection of observable behaviors. Preparedness. Punctuality. Language. Body posture. Follow through. Teamwork is not an attitude. It is listening, contributing, sharing responsibility, and resolving conflict.

When students struggle, it often helps to pause and isolate the skill instead of reacting to the whole situation. A short conversation after a difficult lab or group project can be enough to reset expectations. What went wrong. What the expectation actually is. What one or two specific changes could make a difference next time.

One teacher described using brief reset conversations after tough group days. Over time, students who once avoided responsibility began stepping into leadership roles. Not because they were lectured, but because expectations were made clear and growth was supported.

Building Self-Awareness Through Reflection

Many struggling students are not trying to be difficult. They simply do not realize how their behavior comes across.

Self-awareness is a skill. It has to be taught.

Reflection helps students slow down and evaluate their own actions. Simple prompts used consistently can build emotional Intelligence and accountability over time. Asking students to consider how their attitude affected others, or how a day would have gone if it were a job shift, creates connections they might not make on their own.

Reflection works best when it is not used as punishment. It should feel like practice, not judgment. Over time, students begin to anticipate expectations and adjust behavior before a situation escalates. That is growth.

Relationships as a Foundation for Growth

For some students, the most important employability skill they need to learn first is trust.

Trust that an adult sees their potential. Trust that feedback is meant to help, not embarrass. Trust that effort will be recognized, even when progress is slow.

This does not mean lowering expectations or excusing behavior. It means being consistent. It means holding the line while offering support.

Students need to hear messages like this clearly and often. I am not expecting perfection. I am expecting effort. I will help you improve if you are willing to try.

When students believe that, small wins start to matter. A student who arrives on time two days in a row notice when it is acknowledged. A student who rarely speaks but contributes one idea feels seen. These moments build motivation and a sense of belonging, which are essential for growth.

Progress Over Perfection

No student leaves high school with every employability skill mastered. That is not the goal.

What matters is that students understand what professionalism looks like, have opportunities to practice it, and believe that improvement is possible. Some students take longer to get there. That does not mean the work is failing. It means it is working.

Employers say this consistently. They can teach technical skills. What they need are people who show up, want to learn, and respond to feedback. Those habits are often what separate students who struggle early from those who eventually thrive.

A Student's Story

One CTE teacher shared the story of a student who came into class angry, distracted, and constantly on his phone. Discipline referrals did little to change his behavior.

After one particularly rough lab day, the teacher asked him a simple question. If this were your job, how would your supervisor feel about how today went?

That question changed the tone of the conversation.

Over time, the student began taking reflection prompts seriously. He volunteered for team roles. He still had setbacks, but he also started helping younger students when they struggled. By graduation, he had not only earned his certification, but also a plan for what came next and a strong letter of recommendation from the teacher who once wrote him up regularly.

That transformation did not happen overnight. It happened because expectations were clear, coaching was consistent, and growth was recognized.

Supporting Growth with Structure

Supporting struggling students does not require a new program. It requires intentional structure.

Short reset conversations after conflicts. Reflection prompts that encourage self-evaluation. Tracking small behaviors that build consistency. These tools help students see progress and help teachers stay focused on growth rather than frustration.

When students struggle with employability skills, the answer is not to lower expectations. It is to teach those skills with the same patience and clarity we bring to technical instruction.

That is how students grow into workers others can rely on.

In the next chapter, we will look at another powerful motivator for student growth. Bringing employers into the classroom and using real world expectations to make employability skills visible and meaningful.

Chapter 11

Connecting With Employers

Career and technical education have never been a solo effort. Even the strongest programs struggle when they operate in isolation. Teachers can model expectations, reinforce habits, and coach behavior every day, but employability skills land differently when students hear the same message from someone outside the school building. Someone who hires. Someone who supervises. Someone who has to depend on others to get work done.

When expectations come only from teachers, students sometimes treat them like school rules. When those same expectations come from employers, they start to feel like reality.

That is why employer connections matter so much. Not as a box to check or a compliance requirement, but as a way to reinforce the same behaviors you are already teaching. When school and work speak the same language, students pay attention.

Bringing Employers into the Classroom

You do not need a large job fair or a complicated partnership agreement to make employer involvement meaningful. Some of the most impactful experiences happen in familiar spaces, during regular class time, with clear purpose.

Mock interviews are one example. When students sit across from someone who actually hires people, their posture changes. Their preparation improves. Their listening sharpens. Even students who struggle in the classroom often rise to the moment because the context feels real.

The value is not just in the interview itself, but in the feedback that follows. When an employer comments on communication, preparation, or confidence, students hear it differently. Teachers often notice that students who dismiss classroom feedback take employer feedback seriously.

One teacher told me about a senior who struggled to stay focused during the year. During a mock interview, he was calm, articulate, and prepared. An employer noticed immediately and asked about him afterward. That conversation did more to change the student's attitude than weeks of redirection ever had.

Purposeful Employer Conversations

Panels can be just as powerful when they are focused.

When employers are invited in with no direction, the conversation drifts. When they are invited in with a clear purpose, students lean forward. Asking employers to talk specifically about what they look for in new hires, what separates strong employees from average ones, and when a soft skill made a difference keeps the conversation grounded.

Students ask better questions than we often expect, especially when they know the answers matter. Many want to know what employers learned the hard way, how they handle conflict, and what mistakes cost them opportunities early in their careers. Those stories carry weight.

Preparing students ahead of time helps. Giving them space to submit questions or practice how to ask them builds confidence and reinforces communication skills before the panel even begins.

Using Employer Feedback to Improve Instruction

Employer connections are most effective when they are ongoing, not one-time events.

When industry partners are asked for honest feedback about student readiness, they feel invested. They also tend to be direct. They will tell you where students shine and where gaps show up consistently. That information is invaluable.

Using that feedback closes the loop. When teachers adjust rubrics, update reflection prompts, or reinforce certain behaviors based on what employers say, students begin to see the connection between classroom expectations and workplace reality.

It also builds credibility. Students are more likely to take employ-ability skills seriously when they know those expectations are coming from the field they want to enter.

Seeing the Workplace Up Close

For many students, the workplace remains abstract until they see it. A short visit to a jobsite, clinic, shop, or office can clarify expectat-ions in ways no lesson can. Students notice how people communi-cate, how teams interact, and how problems are handled in real time. They begin to understand that professionalism is not a perfor-mance. It is a daily practice.

When in person visits are not possible, virtual conversations still matter. Employers walking through a typical day, explaining how teams collaborate, or sharing a moment when communication failed can spark meaningful discussion. These stories help students con-nect employability skills to real outcomes.

Reflection after these experiences is critical. Asking students what they observed, what stood out, and what they want to try themselves helps solidify learning and reinforces self-awareness.

Making Advisory Committees Meaningful

Advisory committees have the potential to shape programs in pow-erful ways, but only if they are used intentionally.

Too often, these meetings focus on equipment lists or compliance updates. Shifting part of the conversation to employability skills changes the dynamic. Asking advisory members what behaviors matter most in their hiring process opens the door to honest dialogue.

Inviting them to review rubrics, observe classes, or speak directly with students strengthens alignment. One teacher shared how an advisory member's feedback on student resumes led to clearer expectations and significantly stronger portfolios. That insight did not come from a textbook. It came from experience.

Why Employer Voices Matter

Employers often say the same thing in different ways. Technical skills matter, but initiative, communication, and follow through determine who earns trust. One HVAC business owner described an intern who was technically capable but stood out because of how he showed up early, asked questions, and followed through. Those behaviors led directly to a job offer.

Stories like that resonate with students. They also remind teachers why this work matters, especially on difficult days.

Connecting with employers is not about outsourcing responsibility. It is about reinforcing the message students need to hear from multiple angles. These skills matter. They matter now. And they matter everywhere.

In the next chapter, we will turn our attention to lesson planning and show how employability skills can be integrated intentionally into instruction without overwhelming teachers or diluting technical rigor.

Chapter 12

Integrating Employability Into Existing Lessons

At this point in the book, a reasonable question usually surfaces. This all makes sense. The importance is clear. The strategies feel doable. But how does this actually fit into the lessons I already teach, the standards I already cover, and the time I already do not have?

That concern is not resistance. It is realism.

The good news is that integrating employability skills does not require new units, additional courses, or a second curriculum running alongside the first. Most CTE classrooms are already doing the hardest part. Students are working in teams. They are building, creating, troubleshooting, serving, and presenting. Those activities are already rich with opportunities to develop communication, professionalism, initiative, and problem-solving.

The shift is not about adding more. It is about becoming intentional with what is already there.

When teachers look at lesson plans through the lens of employability, the question changes from "What else do I need to teach?" to

117

"What skills are already showing up here, and how do I make them visible?"

Construction Technology: Learning to Build Together

Consider a construction technology class working on a group build, such as a picnic table. The technical goals are obvious. Students measure, cut, assemble, and follow safety protocols. The project already demands accuracy and skill.

When employability skills are layered in intentionally, the learning deepens. Assigning clear roles such as project manager, materials handler, safety lead, or quality checker gives structure to teamwork. Students begin to understand responsibility beyond their individual task. Using a communication or professionalism rubric during planning and reflection helps students connect their behavior to the outcome of the project.

Weekly reflection journals give students space to think about how they worked together, not just what they built. Teachers often notice that the most valuable moments are not when everything goes smoothly, but when a team has to pause, adjust roles, and problem solve together. That process mirrors the workplace more closely than a flawless final product ever could.

Culinary Arts: Pressure, Timing, and Professionalism

In culinary programs, simulations such as catering a staff appreciation lunch already combine technical skill with real pressure. Timing matters. Coordination matters. Customer expectations matter.

Posting a professionalism rubric and using it daily for self-assessment reinforces habits that carry beyond the kitchen. Role playing customer service scenarios allows students to practice front of house and back of house etiquette before stakes are high. Short pre-shift huddles, led by rotating students, help build communication and leadership skills in a way that feels authentic to the industry.

Employers consistently note that when they hire culinary interns, they pay close attention to how students treat teammates and customers. Knife skills can be taught. Professional conduct takes practice.

Business and Marketing: Feedback and Ownership

In business and marketing classes, projects like developing and pitching a business plan already require creativity, analysis, and presentation. Integrating employability skills strengthens those outcomes.

Using a presentation skills rubric for both peer and teacher feedback helps students understand how their message lands. Work logs that track collaboration, time management, and follow through build accountability. Reflection prompts that ask students to evaluate their pitch as if it were presented to a real client encourage honesty and growth.

Students begin to see feedback not as criticism, but as part of professional improvement. They learn to revise, respond, and present with confidence under deadlines.

Health Science: Human Skills Matter

Health science simulations offer powerful opportunities to teach employability skills because the work is inherently human. Patient intake and bedside manner exercises require more than clinical knowledge. They demand empathy, listening, tone, and composure. Role playing interactions with anxious or frustrated patients allows students to practice responses in a safe environment. Peer review focused on posture, tone, and listening skills helps students become aware of how they come across. Group debriefs give space to discuss what felt real and what could improve.

These moments prepare students for the emotional realities of healthcare work, not just the technical ones.

Agricultural Mechanics: Persistence and Problem Solving

In agricultural mechanics, repairing small engine equipment is a technical challenge that naturally surfaces employability skills. When students face a mystery malfunction, frustration often appears quickly.

Using an initiative checklist shifts attention to how students approach the problem. Do they explore solutions or wait for help? Team based problem solving challenges encourage collaboration and communication under stress. A short bell ringer that asks students to consider how their attitude would appear to a customer watching them work connects behavior to professional reputation.

These experiences teach persistence, adaptability, and real time communication, skills that matter on any jobsite.

A Simple Planning Lens

Across pathways, the pattern is the same. The lesson does not change. The lens does.

Teachers can look at existing plans and ask a few guiding questions. Where does teamwork already happen? Where do students make decisions? Where do communication breakdowns occur? Where could reflection strengthen learning?

Adding rotating roles, brief reflections, peer feedback, or employer scenarios does not disrupt instruction. It clarifies it.

Integration Without Overload

The goal of lesson integration is not perfection. It is consistency. Not every lesson needs to address every employability skill. Over time, however, students should see communication, professionalism, initiative, and accountability reinforced across different contexts. When those expectations show up repeatedly, they become part of the culture.

CTE teachers do not need new lessons. They need new layers. When employability skills are woven into instruction intentionally, students stop seeing them as add-ons and start seeing them as part of the work itself. That is when preparation becomes real.

Part IV

The Classroom Toolkit

Up to this point, the work has been about understanding. What employability skills are, why they matter, and how they already show up in daily instruction. This section is about execution.

At some point, every teacher asks a practical question:

What does this look like when I have students in front of me?

Part IV exists to answer that question without asking you to overhaul your classroom. The tools in this section are designed to support the work you are already doing by making expectations clearer, feedback more precise, and growth easier to see.

Nothing here is meant to be followed exactly as written. These are not scripts or mandates. They are structures you can adapt, combine, and revise to fit your context. Employability skills develop through consistency and clarity, not through complex systems or extra paperwork. A few well-used tools matter more than a full set that never gets revisited.

You will find ways to make employability skills visible through observation, shared language, and reflection. You will see how rubrics and look fors can support coaching without turning behavior into constant grading. You will find conversation structures that help address breakdowns calmly and reinforce growth without escalating conflict.

Use these tools the way you use tools in your shop, lab, or kitchen. Choose what fits. Adjust what doesn't. Revisit what works.

The goal is not perfection.

The goal is consistency.

When employability skills are visible, reinforced, and coached over time, they stop feeling like add-ons. They become part of the work.

Chapter 13

Making Employability Skills Visible

One of the quiet reasons employability skills are so difficult to teach is that they often go unnamed.

Teachers see them every day. Who communicates clearly. Who shuts down. Who takes ownership. Who waits until the last minute and then scrambles. These behaviors are familiar, but familiarity does not automatically lead to clarity. When expectations stay implicit, students are left guessing what actually matters.

Visibility changes that.

Making employability skills visible does not mean adding another layer of evaluation or turning behavior into constant correction. It means helping students see the connection between how they work and what happens because of it. When behaviors are named consistently and tied to outcomes students care about, those behaviors become teachable.

Most classrooms already contain everything needed for this work. The shift is not about adding more. It is about noticing what is already there and choosing to bring it into focus.

Why Visibility Comes Before Assessment

In many schools, employability skills only become visible when something goes wrong. A student misses a deadline. A group falls apart. A conversation escalates. At that point, attention turns to behavior, often through correction or discipline. The message students receive is subtle but powerful: employability skills matter when they fail.

That approach limits growth.

Visibility works best when employability skills are named before they break down. When students hear language about communication, follow through, professionalism, or initiative during normal work, those skills become part of the task rather than a response to misbehavior.

This mirrors how real workplaces function. Supervisors do not wait for failure to talk about expectations. They describe what good work looks like, give feedback along the way, and address issues as patterns emerge. The goal is not control. It is reliability.

Classrooms that make employability skills visible early create the same conditions. Students begin to understand what is being watched, why it matters, and how it affects the work and the people around them.

Seeing Behaviors Instead of Traits

One of the most important shifts in this work is moving away from personality labels and toward observable behavior.

Students are often described as lazy, unmotivated, disrespectful, or irresponsible. Those labels may feel accurate in the moment, but they are not actionable. They do not tell students what to change, and they do not give teachers a clear place to coach.

Employability skills live in behavior, not character.

Communication shows up in whether a student asks a clarifying question before starting. Professionalism shows up in how they respond when corrected. Initiative shows up in whether they take the next step without being prompted. These are things you can see, hear, and describe.

When teachers shift their attention to behavior, conversations change. Feedback becomes more specific. Students are less defensive. Growth becomes possible because the target is clear.

This is the foundation of visibility. If you can see it, you can name it. If you can name it, you can teach it.

Naming What Is Already Happening

Making employability skills visible does not require stopping instruction to deliver a lesson on soft skills. It happens inside the work.

A group struggling to coordinate is a teamwork moment. A rushed project is a time management moment. A defensive response to feedback is a professionalism moment. A student who quietly fixes a problem before it grows is showing initiative.

The opportunity is not to interrupt the work, but to frame it.

Simple statements go a long way:

"This is a communication issue, not a technical one."

"This is what follow through looks like."

"Notice how that decision affected the rest of the group."

When students hear these connections made consistently, they begin to see employability skills as part of the job, not something separate from it.

Over time, they start naming these behaviors themselves. That is when visibility becomes internal rather than enforced.

Making Expectations Explicit Without Overcomplicating Them

Students struggle most when expectations are assumed rather than stated.

In many classrooms, employability expectations live in the teacher's head. The teacher knows what professionalism looks like. The student is expected to figure it out. When they miss the mark, consequences follow, but the expectation itself was never clearly articulated.

Visibility requires clarity.

This does not mean long lists or detailed rules. It means choosing a small number of behaviors to emphasize during a task and stating them plainly.

For example:

"Today I'm paying attention to how you communicate when something doesn't go as planned."

"For this project, follow through matters more than speed."

"I'm watching how teams divide responsibility and support each other."

These statements focus attention without overwhelming students. They also give you something specific to reference during feedback.

Clarity reduces conflict. Students are far more receptive to correction when they understand the expectation in advance.

From Look-Fors to Rubrics: When and How Scoring Makes Sense

This is the point where many educators feel tension.

On one side, employability skills need to be visible and taken seriously. On the other, turning them into constant grades can undermine their purpose. Both concerns are valid.

Rubrics have a place in this work, but only when used intentionally.

At their best, rubrics provide consistency. They help teams of teachers talk about expectations using the same language. They help students understand what growth looks like over time. They support reflection and goal-setting.

At their worst, rubrics turn complex behaviors into checkboxes and encourage students to perform for points rather than develop habits. The difference is not the rubric itself. It is when and how it is used.

Employability rubrics work best after behaviors are already visible. Students need to know what communication, initiative, or professionalism look like in practice before they are asked to evaluate themselves or be evaluated by others.

Scoring too early shifts attention away from learning and toward compliance. Never scoring at all creates ambiguity and inconsistency. The balance lives in using rubrics as reference points rather than constant measures.

Think of rubrics as maps, not meters. They show direction. They help track progress. They are not meant to be consulted every minute.

When rubrics are introduced as tools for reflection and coaching first, scoring becomes less threatening and more meaningful when it does occur.

Using Look-Fors as the Bridge

Before rubrics, there are look-fors.

Look-fors are simple descriptions of observable behavior tied to employability skills. They help teachers notice patterns and help students understand what matters without assigning a number.

For example, instead of scoring "professionalism," you might watch for:

Arriving prepared

Using appropriate language

Responding to feedback without escalation

Maintaining focus during work time

These look-fors guide observation and feedback without turning every moment into an evaluation. They also provide a shared language across classrooms and pathways.

When students hear the same look-fors referenced consistently, they begin to internalize them. That is when behavior starts to change without constant prompting.

Consistency Over Perfection

One of the biggest mistakes teachers make with employability skills is trying to do too much at once.

Visibility does not require tracking every skill during every activity. In fact, that approach often backfires. Students become overwhelmed. Teachers burn out. The work loses focus.

Consistency matters more than coverage.

Choosing one or two employability skills to emphasize during a project creates clarity. Using the same language repeatedly reinforces importance. Revisiting those skills over time builds habits.

This mirrors how learning happens in the workplace. No one expects mastery all at once. Growth comes through repeated attention and adjustment.

What Changes When Skills Are Visible

When employability skills are made visible, several shifts occur. Students stop seeing feedback as personal and start seeing it as performance related. Conversations become calmer. Reflection becomes more honest. Peer expectations rise.

Teachers gain leverage. Instead of reacting to behavior, they coach it. Instead of enforcing rules, they reinforce standards.

Most importantly, students begin to understand that how they work matters just as much as what they produce. That realization changes how they show up, not just in class, but anywhere responsibility exists.

Making employability skills visible is not about control. It is about clarity. And clarity is what allows students to grow.

In the next chapter, we will look at tools that support this work through observation, feedback, and reflection, turning visibility into consistent coaching rather than constant correction.

Chapter 14

Observation, Feedback, and Reflection Tools

Employability skills grow when they are seen, named, and practiced over time. That process does not require complicated systems or constant grading. It requires attention, consistency, and language that helps students understand what their behavior communicates to others.

This chapter focuses on tools that support assessment as coaching. These tools help you notice what matters, respond in the moment, and guide students toward improvement without turning every interaction into a score.

You are already doing much of this work. The difference is intention. When observation, feedback, and reflection are structured just enough, students begin to take ownership of their growth.

Teacher Observation Checklists

Observation is the foundation of coaching. Before you can give useful feedback, you have to notice what is actually happening.

A simple observation checklist helps you focus your attention during labs, group work, simulations, or projects. It keeps feedback grounded in behavior rather than impressions.

An effective checklist is short. It focuses on a small number of employability skills tied to the activity at hand. You might track communication and teamwork during a group build, or professionalism and initiative during independent work.

As you move through the room, you are not looking for perfection. You are looking for patterns. Who starts promptly. Who needs repeated redirection. Who supports others. Who avoids responsibility. Brief notes are enough. A few words capture far more than a number ever could.

These observations give you something concrete to reference during check-ins. Instead of saying, "You need to be more responsible," you can say, "I noticed you waited until the last ten minutes to start. Let's talk about what got in the way."

That shift changes how students receive feedback. It feels fair because it is specific.

Student Self-Reflection Prompts

Self-reflection is where employability skills begin to stick. When students learn to evaluate their own behavior, growth accelerates.

Reflection does not need to be long or emotional. It needs to be honest and regular. Short prompts used consistently are far more effective than occasional deep dives.

Good reflection questions ask students to connect behavior to outcomes. They encourage students to think about how their actions affected the work, the team, and themselves.

Questions like this work well across grade levels and pathways:

What did I do well today when working with others?

What challenged me, and how did I respond?

What would I do differently if this were a job shift?

What skill do I need to work on next?

Over time, patterns emerge. Some students overestimate their performance. Others are overly hard on themselves. Both are teachable moments. Reflection gives you insight into how students see themselves, which helps you coach more effectively.

When reflection becomes routine, students stop seeing feedback as something done to them. They begin to see it as something they use.

Peer Feedback Protocols

Peer feedback reinforces employability skills in a way adult feedback alone cannot. When students give and receive feedback from one another, expectations become shared rather than imposed.

The key is structure. Without guidance, peer feedback can drift into vague praise or unhelpful criticism. With clear prompts, it becomes a powerful learning tool.

Effective peer feedback focuses on observable behavior and specific impact. Students are asked to name what helped the group succeed and what could improve next time. This keeps feedback professional and forward-looking.

Before asking students to give feedback, model it. Show them how to be direct without being personal. Remind them that the goal is growth, not judgment.

Peer feedback also builds empathy. Students begin to understand how their behavior affects others. That awareness carries into future group work and, eventually, the workplace.

Weekly Self-Check Templates

Weekly self-checks help students track growth over time rather than reacting to isolated moments.

These tools work best when they are simple and predictable. Once a week, students pause and rate themselves on one or two employability skills. They note what went well and identify one area for improvement.

This process reinforces that employability skills are developed through practice. It also normalizes struggle. Students see that growth is not linear, and that improvement comes from attention and effort.

For you, weekly self-checks provide valuable context. They help you identify students who need support, students who are ready for more responsibility, and students who may be disengaging quietly. When paired with brief check-ins, these tools turn reflection into action.

Bringing It Together

Observation, feedback, and reflection are not separate tasks. They are parts of the same cycle.

You observe what students do.

You name what you see.

Students reflect on their choices.

Feedback guides the next attempt.

This cycle mirrors how people learn in real workplaces.

Performance is noticed. Feedback is given. Improvement is expected.

When students experience this process consistently in your classroom, they begin to understand that employability skills are not abstract ideas. They are behaviors that can be practiced, adjusted, and strengthened over time.

That understanding prepares them not just for their next job, but for every environment where people work together to get something done.

Chapter 15

Discussion and Coaching Protocols

Teaching employability skills requires more than activities and rubrics. It requires conversations. The kind that are calm, direct, and grounded in purpose. The kind that help students understand how their choices land on others and what they can do differently next time.

As a former school and district leader, I learned this the hard way. The conversations that changed behavior were rarely loud or dramatic. They were steady. They were specific. And they treated people like they were capable of more.

This chapter focuses on coaching protocols that help you respond when things go sideways and reinforce growth when they go right. These are not scripts to memorize. They are structures that keep conversations productive and professional.

Soft Skill Reset Conversations

Every classroom has moments when behavior slips. A student shuts down. A group stops working together. A deadline is missed for the third time.

In those moments, correction alone rarely leads to growth. What works better is a reset conversation that reframes the issue as a performance problem, not a personal flaw.

A soft skill reset starts by naming what happened without assigning motive. You describe the behavior you observed and the impact it had on the work or the team. Then you ask the student to reflect on how that behavior would be viewed in a workplace setting.

The tone matters. This is not a lecture. It is a professional check-in. For example, instead of asking why a student is always late, you might say, "I noticed you came in ten minutes after the task started today and yesterday. When that happens, your team has to adjust. How would a supervisor respond to that pattern?"

That question shifts the focus from blame to awareness. It also invites the student to think beyond the classroom.

A reset conversation should always end with a clear next step. Not a threat. Not a consequence. A plan. What will you try tomorrow? What support do you need? What does improvement look like?

Over time, students learn that mistakes lead to coaching, not labels. That expectation builds trust and accountability at the same time.

Post-Project Debrief Conversations

Projects offer more than technical practice. They offer a chance to reflect on how work actually gets done.

A post-project debrief gives students space to talk about process, not just product. It helps them connect outcomes to behavior.

The most effective debriefs focus on three areas. What worked. What challenged the team. What they would do differently next time.

These conversations work best when you model curiosity rather than judgment. You are not looking for the right answer. You are looking for insight.

Ask students to be specific. General statements like "we worked well together" do not move learning forward. Encourage them to name actions, decisions, and moments.

You might ask, "When did communication breakdown, and what happened next?" or "What choice helped your team stay on track when things got difficult?"

Debriefs are also a chance to reinforce employability language. When students hear words like initiative, follow through, and accountability used in context, those terms begin to mean something.

Over time, students start to anticipate these conversations. They begin thinking about their behavior while they work, not just after the fact.

Using Employer-Style Feedback Language

The language you use matters more than most people realize.

In schools, feedback often sounds academic or disciplinary. In workplaces, feedback sounds different. It is direct. It is specific. And it focuses on impact.

Using employer-style language helps students make the connection between school expectations and workplace expectations.

This means shifting away from phrases like "You need to try harder" and toward language like "Your preparation today affected the quality of the final product."

It also means separating the person from the behavior. Employers rarely say, "You are unmotivated." They say, "The work was incomplete, and that caused a delay."

When students hear feedback framed this way, it feels fairer. It also feels more serious.

You can model this language during class discussions, project feedback, and one-on-one check-ins. Over time, students begin to use it with each other.

That is a sign that employability skills are taking root.

Reflection After Conflict or Failure

Conflict and failure are not interruptions to learning. They are part of it.

What matters is what happens next.

After a conflict between students or a failed project, reflection helps turn frustration into growth. Without reflection, students either shut down or repeat the same patterns.

A structured reflection gives students a way to process what happened without reliving it emotionally.

Start by asking them to describe the situation from their perspective. Then guide them toward analyzing their response. What did they control? What did they not? How did their choices affect others?

Finally, ask them to consider how they would handle a similar situation in a workplace setting.

These conversations take time. They are not always comfortable. But they teach students something many adults never learn how to do.

They learn to pause. They learn to own their role. They learn to adjust.

Those skills matter far beyond your classroom.

Why These Conversations Matter

Employability skills are not built through lectures alone. They are built through repeated experiences where behavior is noticed, discussed, and refined.

The protocols in this chapter help you lead those moments with clarity and confidence. They protect relationships while holding standards. They show students that growth is expected and supported.

When students leave your classroom, they will not remember every project. They will remember how they were treated when they struggled. They will remember whether adults believed they could do better.

That belief, reinforced through calm and purposeful coaching, is one of the most powerful tools you have.

Part V

Bringing it All Together

By this point in the book, nothing here should feel abstract.

You have heard directly from employers across industries. You have seen how employability skills show up in real classrooms, real projects, and real student behavior. You have walked through practical routines, assessment strategies, coaching language, and tools that make this work manageable instead of overwhelming.

Most importantly, you have probably recognized pieces of your own practice along the way.

That matters, because this final section is not about adding something new. It is about naming what already exists, strengthening what already works, and deciding what to do next with intention.

Teaching employability skills is not a program to launch or a box to check. It is a way of seeing your classroom differently. It is the decision to treat behavior as part of learning, not a distraction from it. It is the choice to coach students through how they work, not just whether the work is correct.

This section is where the focus narrows.

Not to perfection. Not to sweeping change. To clarity.

It speaks to teachers who are still trying, even when the work feels heavy. It speaks to leaders who want alignment without another initiative. And it speaks to anyone asking a practical question at the end of a long day: What actually matters, and what should I keep doing tomorrow?

The chapters that follow are not a conclusion so much as a steady landing. They are meant to leave you grounded, affirmed, and clear-eyed about the impact you already have and the small decisions that shape culture over time.

Because long after students forget content, they remember how they were coached, how they were held accountable, and how someone believed they were capable of more.

That work is already happening.

This final section is about carrying it forward.

Chapter 16

A Note to Teachers Who Are Still Trying

If you are reading this at the end of a long day, you are not behind. You are probably tired. Not the kind of tired that a weekend fixes, but the steady fatigue that comes from caring about students in a system that asks a lot and rarely slows down. You are managing safety, standards, equipment, personalities, paperwork, and pressure, often at the same time. You are making dozens of decisions each class period that never show up on a lesson plan or an evaluation form.

That work is real, even when it goes unseen.

CTE teachers, in particular, carry a unique load. You are expected to prepare students for certifications, industry standards, and real workplaces while also meeting academic expectations that were not designed with hands-on learning in mind. You troubleshoot machines, manage materials, calm conflicts, and adjust plans on the fly. You notice who did not eat breakfast. You notice who is frustrated but trying. You notice who is quietly improving, even if no one else does.

None of that shows up neatly in a gradebook.

One of the quiet truths of teaching is that the most important work often feels the least measurable. Coaching a student through frustration. Pulling someone aside after a rough day. Letting a student try again instead of shutting them down. Holding a line while still offering support. These moments are not dramatic. They are not efficient. They do not always feel successful in the moment.

But they are the moments students remember.

When we talk about employability skills, it can sound like one more expectation piled onto an already full plate. Another initiative. Another thing to track. Another set of boxes to check. That is not what this work is meant to be.

Employability skills are not an add-on. They are a reframing of work you are already doing.

When you insist that a student clean their station properly, you are teaching professionalism. When you ask a team to talk through a problem instead of arguing, you are teaching communication. When you expect a student to own a mistake and fix it, you are teaching accountability. When you give feedback that is honest and respectful, you are modeling how adults solve problems at work.

You have been teaching these skills all along, even if you did not always call them by name.

The shift this book invites is not about doing more. It is about being more intentional with what already exists. Naming the behaviors you want students to build. Connecting those behaviors to real expectations beyond school. Giving students language for growth instead of just consequences for mistakes.

This is not about perfection. It never was.

Progress matters more than polish. Consistency matters more than complexity. Culture changes through small moves repeated over time, not through one perfect lesson or a single powerful conversation. A bell ringer that invites reflection. A routine that reinforces responsibility. A moment of feedback that frames behavior as preparation, not punishment.

Those small moments add up.

Students may forget the exact steps of a process years later. They may forget a formula or a definition. But they remember how a teacher spoke to them when they struggled. They remember whether feedback felt like an attack or an invitation to grow. They remember who believed they could do better and showed them how.

Long after graduation, employability shows up in how they handle pressure, how they talk to coworkers, how they respond to feedback, and how they show up when no one is watching. Those habits are shaped slowly, through repetition and example.

You are already part of that process.

This work also allows room for grace. Not every day goes well. Not every class responds the same way. Some students will resist. Some will need far more time than others. Some will take steps forward and then slide back. That does not mean the work is failing. It means it is human.

Teaching employability skills is not about fixing students. It is about coaching them. Coaching takes patience. It takes repetition. It takes the willingness to see behavior as information, not defiance. It asks us to correct without shaming and to hold expectations without giving up on relationships.

That is hard work. It always has been.

If there is one thing to hold onto as you move through the rest of this section, it is this: you do not need to become a different kind of teacher to do this well. You do not need a new personality or a new program. You do not need to overhaul everything at once.

You need permission to start where you are.

Pick one routine. Pick one habit. Pick one skill to emphasize. Name it. Practice it. Talk about it. Reflect on it. Let students try, miss, and try again. Let yourself do the same.

The goal is not to create perfect employees. The goal is to help young people learn how to work with others, manage themselves, and grow into responsibility over time. That happens best in classrooms where expectations are clear, feedback is honest, and effort is noticed.

Those classrooms already exist. Many of them look like yours.

If you are still trying, you are doing meaningful work. And that work matters more than you may ever fully see.

Chapter 17

A Practical Call to Action

At this point in the book, it would be easy to ask you to do everything. To redesign curriculum. To adopt new frameworks. To launch initiatives. To fix problems that have existed longer than any one teacher has been in the classroom.

That is not what this chapter is about.

Change in classrooms does not happen because someone handed teachers a longer list. It happens when teachers make a small number of clear decisions and stick with them long enough for habits to form. That is how culture shifts. Quietly. Slowly. On purpose.

So instead of a checklist, this chapter offers three decisions. Not tasks. Not programs. Decisions you can make with the students you already teach, in the room you already manage, with the time you already have.

The first decision is focus.

You do not need to emphasize every employability skill at once. In fact, trying to do so often waters all of them down. Decide on one skill that matters most for your students right now. Not the one that sounds best on paper, but the one that shows up as a barrier in your classroom.

Maybe it is communication. Students struggle to explain their thinking, ask questions, or speak respectfully under pressure. Maybe it is time management. Deadlines are missed, materials are not ready, and cleanup drags on. Maybe it is teamwork. Group work collapses because students do not know how to share responsibility or resolve conflict.

Choose one. Name it. Let students hear you say it out loud. Tell them this is a skill you will be practicing together this semester because it matters in the workplace and because it matters in this room.

The second decision is routine.

Employability skills grow through repetition, not reminders. Decide on one routine that will anchor the skill you chose. It does not need to be complicated. It just needs to be consistent.

That routine might be a short bell ringer that asks students to reflect on how they communicated the day before. It might be a rotating role during group work that reinforces accountability. It might be a weekly exit reflection that asks students to connect their behavior to workplace expectations.

The key is that the routine happens whether the day goes well or not. Especially when it does not. When routines disappear during busy weeks, students learn that employability skills are optional. When routines stay in place, students learn they matter.

The third decision is language.

Decide that at least once each week, you will talk about behavior, not just work. Not to lecture. Not to shame. To coach.

That moment might happen after a group project falls apart. It might happen during cleanup when frustration shows. It might happen when a student steps up and handles a situation well. What matters is that you name what you are seeing and connect it to life beyond the classroom.

This is where many teachers already do the hardest work without realizing it. They pull a student aside. They ask a question that reframes the moment. They explain why something matters. The difference now is intention. You are not just managing the class. You are building readiness.

When students hear language like, "If this were a job, how would this land?" or "This is the kind of habit employers notice," behavior starts to take on meaning. It stops being about rules and starts being about preparation.

If you made only these three decisions this semester, you would be doing meaningful work.

You would be narrowing your focus instead of spreading yourself thin. You would be building habits instead of chasing compliance.

You would be helping students understand that how they work matters just as much as what they produce.

Tomorrow, when you walk into your classroom, you do not need a new lesson. You need clarity.

Choose the skill. Choose the routine. Choose the moment.

Then do what you already know how to do. Teach. Coach. Adjust. Stay consistent.

That is how change actually happens.

Chapter 18

Using This Book Beyond One Classroom

This book was written with classroom teachers in mind, but the work it describes does not stop at one door. Employability skills grow fastest when students hear the same expectations, language, and feedback across classrooms, pathways, and campuses. When that happens, habits stop feeling situational and start feeling normal.

That is where schools and districts come in.

Part A: For Schools and Districts

For instructional leaders, CTE directors, and principals, this book is not a program to adopt. It is a shared framework that can help bring coherence to work that is already happening in pieces.

Many schools are already talking about professionalism, readiness, or workforce alignment, but those conversations often live in different rooms and sound different depending on who is speaking. One of the simplest ways to strengthen that work is to give teachers a common language and a set of practical reference points. This book can serve that role.

Professional learning communities are a natural place to start. Chapters can be read and discussed over time, not rushed through. A PLC might focus on one employability skill for a grading period and use the examples in Part III to compare how that skill shows up across different classrooms. Those conversations tend to be grounded and productive because they start with practice, not theory. Campus or district professional development can also be anchored in individual chapters rather than broad initiatives. A session on assessment might use the chapter on coaching and feedback as a shared text. A session on classroom culture might center on routines and language rather than discipline systems. Teachers do not need to agree on every detail to benefit from a shared starting point.

The tools in Part IV can support walkthroughs and coaching without turning them into compliance checks. Observation look-fors can help administrators name what they see and give more specific feedback. Reflection tools can be used during coaching conversations to support growth rather than judgment. When leaders and teachers are looking for the same behaviors and using the same language, feedback becomes clearer and more useful.

Perhaps most importantly, employability language creates alignment across campuses. When students hear similar expectations in welding, health science, business, and culinary arts, they begin to understand that these skills are not tied to one teacher or one class.

They are part of how the school prepares them for life beyond graduation.

This work does not require a rollout or a launch. It requires consistency. Leaders who model the language, reinforce the expectations, and protect time for teachers to reflect and adjust will see the impact over time.

Part B: A Final Word About Students

At the center of all of this are students.

They do not arrive with these skills fully formed. Most adults did not either. Employability skills are learned through practice, feedback, and trust. They grow when someone takes the time to coach instead of dismiss, to explain instead of assume.

Students are capable of far more than we sometimes ask of them. When expectations are clear and responsibility is real, they rise. They learn how to communicate. They learn how to manage themselves. They learn how to recover from mistakes and keep going.

Long after students forget the details of a lesson or a project, they remember how they were coached. They remember whether an adult believed they could improve. They remember being trusted with meaningful work.

That is why this work matters.

Not because it prepares students for a specific job, but because it prepares them to navigate whatever work comes next.

Employability skills are not about becoming perfect. They are about becoming capable.

And that is something every student deserves the chance to learn.

Afterword

How We Show Up

This book set out to talk about employability skills, but somewhere along the way, something clearer emerged.

This isn't really about skills lists, rubrics, or frameworks.

It's about how people show up when the work is real.

Across classrooms, jobsites, offices, and organizations, the same patterns keep appearing. People succeed or stall not because of what they know, but because of how they respond when things get hard. How they communicate. How they take responsibility. How they handle feedback. How they adjust when plans change. How they follow through when no one is watching closely.

Those behaviors shape outcomes everywhere.

They shape whether a classroom functions or fractures.

They shape whether a team trusts each other or works around each other.

They shape whether someone grows, gets sidelined, or gets replaced.

For years, we've treated these behaviors as assumed. We expect students to "just know" how to act professionally. We expect new hires to arrive ready. We expect people to figure it out as they go. When they don't, we often label the problem as attitude, motivation, or character.

But what if the issue isn't who people are?

What if it's what they've been taught to practice?

The behaviors we call employability skills are not personality traits. They are learned responses. They are shaped by the environments people move through and the expectations that are made visible to them. When expectations are vague, people guess. When feedback is inconsistent, habits don't form. When responsibility is artificial, growth stalls.

When expectations are clear and the work matters, people rise.

That pattern is playing out quietly all around us. Teachers are naming behaviors instead of punishing them. Employers are coaching instead of replacing. Individuals are realizing that growth doesn't stop when school ends or when a job begins. Learning continues wherever responsibility exists.

This is not a program.

It doesn't belong to one system, one sector, or one title.

It's a shift in how we think about readiness and responsibility.

It's schools acknowledging that they are preparing people to function in real workplaces, not just pass courses.

It's employers recognizing that development doesn't stop at hiring and that feedback is part of leadership, not a failure of it.

It's individuals understanding that how they show up today shapes the opportunities they are trusted with tomorrow.

We don't need to agree on terminology to agree on this.

How we show up matters.

It matters in classrooms when students are trusted with meaningful work and coached through missteps instead of being written off.

It matters in workplaces when expectations are clear and growth is treated as ongoing, not optional.

It matters in lives when people realize they are not finished products, but capable of learning, adjusting, and leading wherever they stand.

You don't need permission to be part of this.

You already are.

Every time you choose to make expectations visible.

Every time you coach behavior instead of labeling character.

Every time you treat growth as something practiced, not possessed.

That's how movements form. Quietly. Practically. Through daily decisions.

This book doesn't end that work.

It points to it.

What happens next depends on how you show up.

About the Author

Dr. Ben Clinton is an educator, leadership coach, and consultant with more than two decades of experience working at the intersection of schools, systems, and the workforce.

Across 21 years in education, including more than 15 years overseeing Career and Technical Education programs, he has worked alongside CTE teachers, campus leaders, and district teams navigating the daily realities of instruction, accountability, and workforce preparation. During that time, he has also spent years listening to employers across industries who consistently raise the same concern: technical skill may get someone hired, but employability skills determine who grows, who is trusted, and who stays.

Ben's career spans classroom teaching, instructional coaching, campus leadership, and district level executive leadership. As a turnaround principal and later as a Deputy Superintendent, he led work that moved campuses from low-performing labels to A ratings by focusing on culture, clarity, and execution rather than short-term fixes. His work is known for being practical, direct, and grounded in how organizations actually function.

Today, Ben is the Founder of Beacon Administrative Consulting, where he partners with schools, municipalities, and organizations to strengthen leadership, improve systems, and build workforce readiness. His work includes professional development, executive coaching, strategic planning, and training that helps educators teach the behaviors employers expect without turning classrooms into compliance-driven environments.

Ben holds a Bachelor's degree in Economics from Rice University and a Doctor of Education in Educational Leadership from Lamar University. He is a John Maxwell Certified Coach and an active speaker focused on leadership, culture, and workforce readiness.

He wrote *Teaching What Every Employer Wants* to give CTE teachers a clear, practical way to teach the habits that make technical skills usable, and to help students leave school ready not just to get hired, but to last, grow, and lead.

Learn more at Beacon345.com.

www.ingramcontent.com/pod-product-compliance
Lightning Source LLC
Chambersburg PA
CBHW071515140726
47997CB00005B/1973